2024–2025 EDITION

9th GRADE READY

EXPERT ADVICE TO HELP PARENTS
NAVIGATE THE YEAR AHEAD

BY
TIMOTHY M. DOVE
AND MEMBERS OF THE NATIONAL NETWORK
OF STATE TEACHERS OF THE YEAR

A READY GUIDE

PARENT **READY!**

PARENT **READY**

2024-2025 Edition

Published by Parent Ready
8 E. Windsor Avenue
Alexandria, Virginia 22301
https://parentready.com

Parent Ready and design are trademarks of Parent Ready, Inc.

The publisher is not responsible for websites (or their contents) that are not owned by the publisher.

ISBN: 979-8-9865331-6-2 (paperback)
ISBN: 979-8-9865331-8-6 (e-book)

Bulk purchases: Quantity discounts are available. Please make inquiries via https://schoolready.guide.

Table of Contents

This series of books is dedicated to all those who contribute to the education and support of young people. I was lucky enough to be a classroom teacher for 32 years. I owe a lot of my effectiveness to those who worked with me and those who taught me so much over the years, especially two master educators, Jenelle and Mark Dove, my parents. We all have teachers we think back on who made important contributions to our formal and informal education. Our parents and classroom teachers are on the front lines to encourage, question, teach, and celebrate our students. I want to thank all my colleagues who agreed to be a part of this project. We can always learn from one another, and having many voices in this conversation is so helpful. Thank you to all the educators who are still engaged in this sacred trust.

—Timothy M. Dove

Contributors

Editor

Timothy M. Dove, an educator for 42 years, is the Ohio State Teacher of the Year in 2011 and 2012. Tim was a middle school teacher for 32 years and helped develop the Global Scholars Diploma program. He taught high schoolers for three years, was an adjunct professor at The Ohio State University for 20 years, and for the past decade has worked with state and national education agencies supporting educators and students in a variety of ways. He has been a consultant with Battelle for Kids in Hong Kong, Learning Forward, the Council of Chief State School Officers (CCSSO), and the Collaboration for Effective Educator Development, Accountability, and Reform (CEEDAR) Center.

Contributors

Bethany Bernasconie is the 2012 New Hampshire Teacher of the Year, a 2013 ASCD Emerging Leader, a 2014 Milken Fellow, and a 2017 School ReTool Fellow. After earning a BA in Biology and a MAT in Secondary Science Education, both from Boston University, she began teaching high school in 2004 in Lincoln-Sudbury, Massachusetts. In 2009, she helped to open the doors of Windham High School, where she taught Biology and was the Director of Science and Engineering 6-12 for the Windham School District. From 2015-2022, she was honored to serve as the Assistant Principal and then Principal of Amherst Middle School in New Hampshire. In 2017, she completed her doctorate in Curriculum, Instruction, and Assessment through Walden University. Her doctoral research focused on closing the gender achievement gap in STEM through building and implementing cognitive apprenticeships in secondary school communities of practice. Currently, Bethany is a Leader-in-Residence with 2Revolutions.

Heidi Crumrine is an English teacher and literacy coach at Concord High School in Concord, New Hampshire, where she has taught since 2004 after teaching three years in the New York City Public School system. The 2018 New Hampshire Teacher of the Year, Heidi's writing has been published in the *Concord Monitor, Education Post*, blogs for Teaching4Tomorrow, Heineman, and the National Network of State Teachers of the Year. Her students' work has been featured on New Hampshire Public Radio and the We Are America Project. Heidi serves on the board of Reaching Higher NH. She is the author of *50 Strategies for Reluctant Readers* published by Shell.

National Board-Certified **Heidi Edwards** has taught for 23 years. She teaches physical science, Advanced Placement biology, botany, and biotechnology at Oakwood High School in Oakwood, Ohio. She is active in her school culture as science department chair, teacher mentor, student council advisor, and cheer coordinator. Her passion for STEM led to opportunities to fly high-altitude missions aboard NASA's SOFIA observatory and selection as a 2023–24 CDC Science Ambassador fellow. Heidi served Air Camp USA as the curriculum specialist, leading to recognition as the 2012 National Air Force Association Teacher of the Year runner-up and the 2018 National Aviation Hall.

Lorynn Guerrero is an assistant principal at Gadsden High School in Anthony, New Mexico. She taught English to 9th- and 10th-grade students for 13 years before transitioning into the administrative role. She is the 2022 New Mexico Teacher of the Year and a New Mexico Teach Plus Policy Fellow for the 2022-23 year. She previously taught teen parents in a GRADS (graduation, reality, and dual-role skills) program that supported them in earning their high school diplomas. Before that, she taught 9th- through 11th-grade English at Organ Mountain High School in Las Cruces for five years. She began her teaching career in Hatch, New Mexico, teaching 6th-grade English and received her first nomination for Teacher of the Year in 2008. Lorynn has a master of education with an emphasis in education administration, a bachelor of science in secondary education with an emphasis in English language arts, Advanced Placement certification in literature and composition, and Teaching English to Speakers of Other Languages certification (TESOL). In December 2022, she received an award for Outstanding Student in Education Administration from Eastern New Mexico University. She was nominated for *Tú Revista Latina* magazine's Educators for Excellence award. Her pedagogical priority is to encourage personalized education for all students.

Barbara J. Hopkins, PhD, grew up in Nebraska and always knew she wanted to be a teacher. She taught English to middle school students in rural and urban schools, served as a reading specialist, and served as a school administrator who turned around schools that were challenged. The key for her, in education and life, is always showing you care and doing your best to help. Barbara is a Nebraska State Teacher of the Year and Nebraska Christa McAuliffe Award winner for courage in education. She has been honored nationally with numerous awards for her dedicated service. Middle school is her favorite grade span to teach, because it sets the stage for students to succeed in high school and find the path to their future.

Joan Hurley, the 2008 Connecticut Teacher of the Year, has been an educator and advocate for children and families in Connecticut's public urban and magnet school districts for 33 years. Since 1990, Joan has served Hartford Public and Capitol Region Education Council Magnet Schools. CREC, an intentionally diverse social justice organization, attempts to affirm and honor the experiences of all students and families, and willingly challenge inherited beliefs and ideologies to create a more harmonious, integrated world. Joan, passionate about the intersections of justice, equity, and education, is an advocate, disruptor, learner, listener, teacher, writer, reader, mom, empath, and horse owner–envier. She loves picture books and popcorn, though not necessarily in that order.

Carolyn Kielma is the 2023 Connecticut Teacher of the Year and a 2023 National Teacher of the Year finalist. Since 2002, she has taught the love of science to students in Connecticut, and currently teaches 6th-grade science at Bristol Arts & Innovation Magnet School. She taught biology, anatomy & physiology, biotechnology & forensics, and Advancement Via Individual Determination (AVID) at Bristol Eastern High School for 15 years prior. Carolyn believes that teaching is not only about the curriculum, but also helping youth become better humans. Her goal is to provide an inclusive environment where all students feel valued, accepted, and treated with equity. She believes learning is not about knowing the right answer; it is a process of discovery. Carolyn works to close the opportunity gap by preparing all students for college and career readiness and success in a global society.

Mandy Manning, the 2018 Washington State and National Teacher of the Year, advocates for educators, public schools, and students as the digital content specialist for the Washington Education Association. She served 21 years in the classroom as the first teacher for newly arrived refugee and immigrant students at Ferris High School in the Newcomer Center in Spokane, Washington. She serves on several education-related boards, including the Spectrum Center Board, serving the LGBTQ+ community in Spokane. Mandy is co-author of *Creating a Sense of Belonging for Immigrant and Refugee Students: Strategies for K-12 Educators*. Her book, *50 Strategies for Teaching Multilingual Learners*, will be published by Teacher Created Materials in spring 2024.

Stacey McAdoo, 2019 Arkansas Teacher of the Year, is the executive director for Teach Plus Arkansas. Previously, she spent 19 years in the Little Rock School District as an accomplished classroom practitioner, college and career readiness coordinator, and lead secondary novice mentor teacher for the entire district. As a professional development facilitator for more than two decades, she designs and leads sessions that focus on best practices, instructional strategies, empowerment of student and teacher voice, and promotion of equity and the success of diverse learners. Stacey is the founder of The Writeous Poets (a spoken word and youth advocacy collective), a board member of the Central Arkansas Library System, and a member of the National Arts in Education Advisory Council. Stacey holds a BA in professional and technical writing, an MA in teaching, and an EdS in curriculum, instruction, and assessments. She lives in Little Rock with her husband, Leron, and they are the proud parents of Norel and Jamee. Visit her blog at www.stillstacey.com to learn more about her.

Al Rabanera, is a high school math educator and educational leader from La Vista High School in Fullerton, California. Al also serves as the lead teacher for STEAM and Academy, where he played a key role in developing an award-winning Social-Emotional Learning (SEL) program that boosted student confidence and engagement, and even earned the Golden Bell Award in 2023. Al has advocated for educators, previously serving as a Board of Director for the Institute for Teaching and the Council for Accreditation of Educator Preparation. In 2017, he was one of five educators to receive the Horace Mann Award for Teaching Excellence. Al is also a Global Learning Fellow and a Distinguished Alumni of his alma mater, California State University Fullerton. Al has influenced education policy as a Teach Plus California Policy Fellow and Senior National Policy Advisory Board Member. When he's not inspiring young minds, Al enjoys time with his wife, Cassandra, and their children, Nehemiah and Aurora.

Jada Reeves, 2019 West Virginia State Teacher of the Year, is an academic coach for Raleigh County Schools in southern West Virginia. Before she began her current job assignment, she was a 5th-grade teacher, a Title I reading teacher for 10 years, and a kindergarten teacher. Jada graduated from Concord College with a bachelor of science in elementary education K-6 and went on to earn a reading specialist master's degree, a National Board Certification in literacy and language for early and middle elementary school, and an administrator's certificate. Jada is pursuing a doctorate through Walden University in curriculum, instruction, and assessment. Jada is an online facilitator for the eLearning for Educators program through West Virginia Department of Education (WVDE). She is the lead coordinator for the Southern WV National Board Certification cohort through the WVDE and serves as one of its facilitators for awareness in certification. She is actively involved in the WV division of the Elevating and Celebrating Effective Teaching and Teachers and is a member of the planning committee. Jada contributes to the National Board for Professional Teaching Standards blog, *The Standard.*

Tiffany Richard was the 2012 Kansas State Teacher of the Year and the first winner of the Kansas University Excellence in Teaching award, after being nominated by a former student in 2006. During her 28-year education career, she has taught a variety of science courses at the secondary level in the states of California, Kansas, and Texas. Her favorite course is 9th-grade biology, because she loves the energy and enthusiasm of 9th graders. She also coordinated the AVID program, a high school college preparatory program, for 10 years in Olathe, Kansas. This program worked with students to provide the skills and support needed for success in advanced courses to prepare them for college success. Currently, she is using her master's in curriculum and instruction as an instructional coach in Katy, Texas, where she works with secondary science teachers to improve their science instruction. While she enjoyed teaching at the same school that her son and daughter attended, she is most proud to currently be working at the same school as her son—a 9th-grade English teacher.

Jim Shaner is a National Board-Certified science and STEM teacher who has taught in the Greenon Local School District in Ohio for 24 years. He has a master of science teaching degree and a master of education degree from Wright State University. He enjoys teaching physical science, robotics, drones, and computer-based STEM classes and is looking to move into administration to foster increased change in education.

Jennifer Skomial has been completely obsessed with the teaching profession since she was in 1st grade. She began by teaching English for the first six years of her career, in middle and high school settings. During the ten years that followed, Jennifer taught high schoolers in the Academy for Education and Learning at a vocational-technical high school, preparing them for future careers as teachers and other educational fields. In 2019, Jennifer was selected as the New Jersey State Teacher of the Year, an honor that provided many opportunities to hone her leadership abilities and professional experiences. During this time she was afforded a sabbatical from teaching and worked for the New Jersey Department of Education as a spokesperson for educators across the state and country. She began her current, and most rewarding, role as an elementary principal in 2023. During her free time, Jennifer can be found spending time with her family (which includes three future teachers) and working toward a Doctorate in Education.

Dr. John Skretta, 2017 Nebraska Superintendent of the Year, is the chief administrator for Educational Service Unit 6, headquartered in Milford, Nebraska, which delivers professional development, student services, and technology infrastructure and support to 16 public school districts across five counties. Prior to serving in his current role, John was a superintendent, assistant superintendent, and high school principal. He began his education career as a high school English teacher.

Foreword

John Skretta
2017 Nebraska Superintendent of the Year

The 9th-grade experience is one of the most pivotal yet precarious moments in the educational path of a student. As a longtime building and school district administrator who now works at a regional level with 16 different school districts, I continue to marvel at the myriad ways in which the freshman year bears its unique set of challenges and opportunities for students, parents, and the educators who serve them. Across the years, a consistent observation I've made—and a truism affirmed by colleagues across our high schools—is the turning-point impact of the 9th-grade experience. It is a year of transition, a year that can bring with it both triumphs and turmoil for students and their loving parents and guardians, who long for their children to succeed but sometimes feel perplexed about how to help them do so. It is in the 9th grade, perhaps more than any of the secondary years, where pathways diverge: Students who succeed as freshmen tend to flourish in the remaining high school years, which puts them on a pathway to postsecondary success as well. Sadly, students who stumble out of the gate in the 9th-grade year may fail to realize their potential.

More than 20 years ago, in one of my first educational leadership roles, I served as a co-coordinator for the 9th-grade class of a large and diverse high school in Lincoln, Nebraska. As part of our work, we applied for and won a large education innovation grant to provide more systemic transition supports for incoming freshmen. I'd like to say we won this competitive state grant based upon my persuasive writing skills, but I think it was much simpler than that: The needs analysis demonstrated we had a crisis on our hands, with almost half of our 9th-grade students experiencing failure in one or more courses. We worked diligently as a grant team of school administrators and lead teachers to partner with area feeder middle schools to strengthen lines of communication and formalize 9th-grade orientation processes in order to provide a more positive experience for incoming freshmen. We used grant resources to monitor attendance and provide earlier interventions through parental contacts and outreach for freshmen students who were habitually tardy or chronically absent. We identified groups of incoming 9th graders who were deemed to be most at risk of academic failure or social setbacks based upon identified criteria and middle school-level performance. Once we had established the referral process, we created a wraparound, team-based support of additional parental contacts, counselor check-ins, and academic assistance. Not surprisingly, we learned that attendance, academic achievement, and students' self-reported sense of productivity and success were enhanced by bringing these measures to them right up front.

My days of working closely with that student cohort and the families in the neighborhoods of northeast Lincoln are now long past. As the years have gone by, I've served in a wide variety of roles in different settings, from assistant principal to principal and eventually school district superintendent. From every vantage point throughout my career, I can assure you that the 9th-grade experience is a bellwether for future success, and this is a remarkably consistent truism in schools big and small and in locations rural and urban.

Make no mistake; 9th grade can be daunting. It can be a year where inevitable challenges, both in the classroom and outside of it, cause students to flounder and sometimes fail. Yet it can also be a year where aspiration and ambition gel to make it a launching pad for the future.

It is often a year when young people form more future-oriented goals and find that sustained effort can lead to tremendous outcomes: success in the classroom, competitive excellence on the field or court, thriving peer relationships through cocurricular involvement in student clubs, and positive social connections through high school relationships.

This book will help families and students (as well as educators working with 9th graders) ensure that the odds of success for the 9th-grade year are leaning in their favor. This book is a gift! It is the gift of empowerment, because reading it and putting these words into action will lead to greater self-directedness and self-efficacy for our students. Through the words, insights, and actionable advice of the experts who have written these chapters, parents will be better able to help their children navigate the 9th-grade journey to bright future horizons.

Introduction

Timothy M. Dove
2011 & 2012 Ohio State Teacher of the Year

This book is for the parents, family members, caregivers, siblings, mentors, and other supporters of a soon-to-be 9th grader. Think of these narratives as advice from a friendly teacher in your child's school.

For those of you embarking on the new or repeated experience of having a high schooler in your family, you'll find loads of information useful to you and your student.

Each contributor to *9th Grade Ready* is a current or former 9th-grade educator who has worked extensively with parents and families. These contributors have all been Teachers of the Year, finalists for the award, or otherwise recognized on the state level for their abilities in the classroom. They are experts in 9th grade and in the topics of the chapters they penned.

Those chapters cover many of the topics that you may be thinking about as your child enters 9th grade. Beginning with how 9th grade differs from 8th and moving through preparation for 10th grade, this book will serve as your guide. It will describe what to expect in a variety of areas and things to look for as you navigate your child's physical, emotional, and academic growth. This book focuses on both action items and tips on how to support your child as they* start finding their independence. Some information might seem obvious, while other pieces will be eye-opening. Every family is different, and parts of the book will resonate differently with each reader. The new information can help you plan, and the things you already know should assure you that you are on the right track.

Most chapters give prompts or conclude with a list of conversation starters. In thinking about how to use them, consider your relationship, family dynamics, and student's history. Using open-ended questions is the best way to get information from your student. Not only will having these conversations assist you in supporting your child, but they will also open new lines of communication that can continue throughout the school year.

This book can be used in different ways. You can focus on the chapters needed or of interest based on timing, or you can read it straight through to get a sense of the overall landscape in order to spark ideas.

Ninth grade is a major year of change for your child. We hope this book helps you navigate it.

*The pronoun they/them is used in its singular form throughout the book because it is the most practical and inclusive approach.

Chapter 1

HOW IS 9TH GRADE DIFFERENT FROM 8TH GRADE?

Ways to support your student with high school expectations

Lorynn Guerrero
2022 New Mexico State Teacher of the Year

As a 9th-grade English teacher, I have been fortunate to work with this group of students and their families for 10 years. While many teachers groan about working with high school freshmen, I love it. During a recent job interview, I was told I would be teaching freshmen. I clapped my hands together, and said, "Yes! Those are my peeps!" I was happily hired for the position.

I enjoy working with freshmen because they still have that thirst for knowledge and are excited about their new school, but at times they can be intimidated by their new surroundings. Sometimes, 9th-grade students are still at junior high, but in the districts I've taught in New Mexico, 9th grade is the first year of high school. The high school setting has more students and the students in your child's classes can range from age 13 to 19 (more about this on page 10). The campuses may be larger to include more teachers and more support staff. The lunches may be divided into A and B lunches. There may be four or five different academic counselors who call students out of class to check on academic progress. There are so many different things to which these new students have to become acclimated. Students are going through a lot of changes, physically, mentally, and emotionally.

There are many new experiences a 9th grader will encounter during high school. Remember that this transition is a learning experience for your student *and* yourself. Even if you have gone through a 9th-grade year with an older child, every child is different. As a parent of two, I watched my sons grow up in the same house, while being two totally different human beings.

Communication

One thing to do is to **keep the lines of communication open**. Understand that it is really difficult when a child starts to keep things from you or even lies about certain things. I see students lying out of fear that they're going to get in trouble. When I work with my students, I feel uncomfortable when I know that they are keeping things from their parents by not being honest about their struggles. Parents are often in the dark about their child's academic progress or social aspects of school. New friends and acquaintances can play a huge role in what motivates your child or what drives them to procrastination. I see students wanting to focus on the social aspects of making new friends and being influenced by other students. These influences can be both positive and negative. I wanted to know who my children's friends were. I would encourage my children to invite their friends to our house for meals or to hang out.

Attendance

Parents must contribute to the transition from middle school to high school. Most 9th graders have a great attendance rate because they don't yet have a driver's license or personal vehicle to drive off campus and ditch classes. Families usually make sure their child gets on the bus. They may even drop off their student at school in the morning.

Many students know they are required to attend all their classes throughout the day. There are two types of absences. There is an *excused absence,* when the student is out for an appointment. The family is aware of the absence, and there is documentation of the student being out of class. It is the student's responsibility to get their makeup work and turn in any missing assignments. The second type of absence is an *unexcused absence.* That is when there has been no type of notification to the school that the student will not be in class. The penalties are more severe if a student has unexcused absences. Parents can be held accountable and even fined by county truant officers. Many times, parents feel that an excused absence is okay. In reality, students should be in class 90% of the school year. Most 9th graders haven't picked up on the notion of "skipping classes" yet or casually attending a lunch time other than the one assigned to them.

Expectations

I use the first few weeks at the beginning of the new school year to explain to students my expectations, which is one way to motivate them to do well in 9th grade. I tell them that an assignment due date is set. Students cannot turn in assignments months, or even days, late. I explain that, in the real working world, a boss is going to ask for something to be done. If they're continually late in finishing a project, they could be fired. I set this expectation from the very beginning. I also expect my students to be ready to work and have all their supplies once the bell rings. Again, I tie it to real job expectations—a boss will not appreciate tardiness. I do take into account all the things that happen to students on their way to class, but again, I expect them to keep the lines of communication open with me. They have to talk to me, just like they would a supervisor at a job, and tell me what's going on so we can work together. Of course, I take the student's needs into consideration as well, like their IEPs or their 504s.

I've learned over the years that I cannot assume students always know how I'm interpreting a topic. This is going to be the same for parents, too—don't assume your child knows what you're thinking. Being specific about your expectations is very important. Talk to your student about maintaining passing grades. In high school, that can mean earning Cs. Many families are used to their middle school child earning straight As. However, in high school, the expectations for learning increase drastically. The coursework is going to be more challenging. Students will be asked to work more independently. They will have to complete homework in a timely manner. Deadlines will be enforced, and excuses will not be accepted by teachers.

Depending on what works best for your family, having a schedule that maps out times, dates, and activities is very helpful. While I know we live in the 21st century, there is something about having an actual tangible calendar that the family can refer to. This calendar can be kept in an area where everyone sees the family's activities and events. At my house, that family calendar is still up, even though my sons are in college. It includes due dates for their assignments and game days. I'm fortunate that they still share their class syllabi with me, so I can ask them how their assignments are going. In addition to having something that is tactile, you can also use the calendar on your cell phone. That way, notifications can be instantaneous, and parents and students can know what activities or homework assignments are coming up.

It is hard to stay on top of your child's every event, but in order for students to be successful and motivated, these expectations have to be set at the beginning of the school year. Ask your child if their teachers have provided a class syllabus. There may be due dates and assignments on there that can be put into the family calendar to help alleviate some of the stress of doing assignments and projects at the last minute.

High School Credits

Some freshmen have a hard time understanding that the credits they earn in high school are required in order to graduate. I spend a lot of time explaining that these high school credit expectations are very strict. Many times, while giving my speech, upperclassmen who did not learn that lesson and are taking my freshman English class again will nod in agreement. Sometimes they'll interject that the newer students need to listen to me. Depending on the state's requirements, students have to earn a certain number of credits to graduate. These required classes can include physical education, health, and a year of a foreign language. Spend some time reading your high school's course selection handbook and discuss the choices with your child. Let them know that you understand how hectic their new schedule may be, but encourage them to choose some electives that interest them. Emphasize the importance of this first year, including learning the class material and passing the classes to earn credit.

Work with the teacher. Many times, I have felt that parents blamed me because their child failed the first semester of freshman English, or worse still, the whole year. A lot of students are successful in middle school, but at the high school level, the work becomes more challenging, and students do struggle. You can support your student, and the teacher, by contacting the teacher and saying, "I can see that my child is struggling. What can I do at home to support my child so they are successful in your classroom?" Many schools have parent portals that give parents access to their student's grades in real time. If you have access to your student's grades, you can spark a conversation with your child by asking, "I noticed you have a zero in your class; how are you going to make up that grade?" That way, the student is aware that you're seeing their grades and will be less likely to lie about the issue.

Extracurricular Activities

If you see your child starting to get behind, know that it is okay to have them sit out a practice or two to get caught up on their classwork. This is a new consequence that they may not be used to. It only takes a few times before your student realizes that you are serious about classwork, and that extra activities come second. It is a hard reality when your child becomes ineligible to participate in extracurricular activities. Coaches and sponsors are very strict about this policy, because having an ineligible participant can mean a forfeit of games or activities they've won. In New Mexico, the state has requirements for student expectation through the New Mexico Activities Association. These activities include sports and clubs like theater, e-sports, etc. Any group that participates in a state championship is required to follow the rules. The expectation is that students have a 2.0 GPA and no Fs in order to participate in the activity.

There is also a school attendance rule tied to the expectation. As previously mentioned, students should be in attendance at least 90% of the time. The coaches and sponsors know these expectations and will not hesitate to sit out students who are failing. It will not matter if the child is very skilled at the activity; they will still have to sit out.

There are also the coaches' expectations and commitment to the sport. High school coaches require students to be at practices during holidays and nonschool days. Sometimes the coaches will penalize students for going on family vacations during spring break or the summer. My sons are five years apart, so, for 10 years, we did not take family vacations during spring break or summer. Our Thanksgiving and winter breaks were filled with winter sports and team tournaments, not holiday destinations.

Work with the coaches and sponsors to support your student if they are struggling in class. It will also show your child the partnership between you and the coach/sponsor. My son's wrestling coach and I worked together, for example, to help improve my son's grades and set the expectation that school is important. My son had several Fs in his sophomore classes. Instead of wrestling, he had to catch up on his work during practice time. If his grades weren't passing, he wouldn't have had the opportunity to compete at the state wrestling competition. He wanted to travel to compete, so he talked to his teachers to get his assignments completed and worked for two weeks to improve his grades.

Teacher Appreciation

If your 9th-grade student is in a new school with new teachers, new administrators, and new expectations, remember that everyone is learning at the same time. Some schools have a large number of students. While the classroom teachers try their best to educate your child, they may have large class loads. Sometimes, a teacher can have up to 30 students in a class for six different class periods. At times, parents may think that a teacher does not care about their students, but I care a lot about the success of mine. Many times, as I'm grading, I will take time to look up the student's grades and call their parents to tell them their student is struggling. It takes more time for me to finish grading this way, but I feel it is important to ask families how we can work together to help the student get on track with their schoolwork. Please allow for a little bit of grace as teachers work through grading assignments.

Being a high school teacher is a lot different than being an elementary teacher. Think about offering a high school teacher assistance, like you used to do in elementary school. While your child may not think it's cool, the teacher might be very grateful. Items for the classroom are always appreciated. Even helping teachers put up bulletin boards is helpful. I love when a parent helps me with things in my classroom, and I always welcome parents to come and speak to my students about their careers. Find ways to get involved in the classroom—it may shock the teachers! Some teachers may politely reject your offer, but making the offer is still powerful.

Exposure to Older Students

Some high school students can be as old as 18 and 19 years old. In the traditional 9th-grade English/language arts curriculum, I teach William Shakespeare's *Romeo and Juliet*, about two young characters. They like one another, but their parents don't like the other family. I tell my students that, as new kids in high school, they will encounter people their parents won't like. The main idea I want students to take away from the tragedy is that the lines of communication need to stay open. Had the characters talked to their parents, a lot of the misconceptions and tragedies that occurred could have been avoided.

I talked to my children and asked about the people they hung out with. It's hard to do it judgment-free for parents, but your young adults are learning how to navigate high school life. I was always involved in my children's activities or booster clubs. I interacted with their teammates and their teammates' parents. I made some great friends this way, and it helped me be involved in what my children were doing and who they were hanging out with. When the kids were hanging out at one another's homes, it helped that I knew the parents and had been invited into their homes. We often shared pictures of the activities they were doing, which enabled me to have conversations with my children when they came home about what they did. It made it easier because I knew who they were talking about, especially because some of the students my children liked were older. Being involved in your child's activities helps to motivate them. It becomes a family activity that everyone is involved in.

Closing Advice

I often tell my students' parents, "Transitioning from a middle school to a high school setting is difficult for everyone. Understand that your children are going through a lot of changes. Don't get upset or disappointed. During this time, you'll need to help guide them through the transition."

Remember that nothing has to be perfect. Ninth grade is the foundation of your student's high school career, and, while you need to plant the seeds for what comes after high school, it is most important for your freshman to have fun in high school. That is what makes it memorable.

Conversation Starters

- Tell me about your new teachers and their expectations for you in their classroom.

- How far are your classrooms from each other? Have you been navigating the new school okay?

- What do your classes look like? How many students are in them?

- What is one thing a teacher said today that got your attention?

- What is one thing that made your day?

Chapter 2

TEACHER EXPECTATIONS IN 9TH GRADE

How scaffolding supports high expectations

Joan Hurley
2008 Connecticut State Teacher of the Year

"When I was a boy of 14, my father was so ignorant I could hardly stand to have the old man around. But when I got to be 21, I was astonished at how much he had learned in seven years."
—Mark Twain

The physical, social, emotional, and intellectual transformations that occur during adolescence resonate with parents and children in ways that are distinct from any other time in their lives. Teens' bodies are a bounty of hormones and growth spurts. Emotions are up, down, and all around—and woe to the parent who says the wrong thing at the wrong time! As this developmental cacophony merges with the transition from 8th grade to the first year of high school, adolescents are fueled by competing emotions (feeling anticipatory, withdrawn, excited, ambivalent...). They attempt to define who they are as individuals while simultaneously claiming a group identity—a teen subculture—as their own. At this stage, parents often feel like they've been kicked to the curb, relegated to being outside observers who are desperately trying to find their way back in.

To parents of freshmen, this evolution from the effusive awkwardness of the middle school preteen to the typical monosyllabic 9th-grade reserve may seem sudden and suspicious. Ninth graders practice at home how to be offended by the boorish (that'd be *you*, parents!). Well-intentioned advice will be actively scorned as a didactic affront to emerging identity. If parents foolishly offer a gem of sincere guidance in public, 9th graders will distance themselves with overt and covert gestures of disdain and embarrassment. Some will respond with argument for the sake of argument. Parental disagreement will be interpreted by teens as misinterpretations of themselves, betrayals of their identities, or criticisms of the adolescent subculture they have embraced and seek acceptance from.

It is important to remember that, if your adolescent is surly about your advice or doesn't want to be seen with you, you *have not failed* in your role as a parent! While the ego-boosting adoration that younger children and preteens exuded in the past has been seemingly reduced to brief *hellos*, perfunctory hugs, and dismissive shrugs, it must be noted that 9th graders' demands for parental distance is developmentally appropriate.

So. How *do* parents of 9th graders support and guide their children while also pretending to hide under a rock? How do parents continue to positively influence their adolescents in the home and at school while honoring the independence they demand? How do parents avoid the dreaded teen accusations of being "intrusive" or "controlling" without feeling like they've succumbed to the mercurial will of their adolescents' angst?

Take heart! It *is* possible not only to survive the middle school to high school transition with your teen, but also to successfully support their journey to becoming a mature, autonomous, happy person who is able to contribute to society in meaningful ways. You can create and provide a flexible structure for building a trusting relationship with your teen, be responsive to their expressed and unexpressed needs, convey encouragement, and have high expectations in their abilities and potential.

Scaffolded Support

Parents must see themselves as facilitators of their teens' progress through 9th grade and beyond. Adolescents need guides who will embrace and flexibly support them as they navigate the rite of passage that is freshman year. Like builders who erect scaffolds to build sky-scrapers, parents must provide scaffolds—steps that are continually adjusted to the trajectory of their child's growth and development—for their adolescents to climb. Similar to construction workers, parents may often feel like they are on the outside looking in. Yet, in this position, they are able to build the steps for their teen to climb toward independence: physical, social, emotional, and intellectual. These scaffolds will be invisible, of course, and provided to adolescents while parents remain hidden and lurking under that proverbial rock, but they will be a reliable system of support, nonetheless.

Freshmen have just emerged from the perception that they are children preparing for young adulthood to actually *being* young adults. As they enter high school, they will respond to this altered perception with reticence, enthusiasm, or some attitude in between. Increased expectations can be intimidating. Freshmen will be culture-scanning their new environment in order to determine how to fit in. Their inner lives are on the developmental path of egocentric veneration. They are fascinated by their daily appearance and preoccupied with peers who, like them, strive to determine what to enthusiastically emulate or flatly rebuff. Yet they are also responsive to pertinent lessons about universal issues and can become deeply invested in finding solutions to problems in the greater world—if they are trusted to do so at their own pace and in their own way. With scaffolded support, it's possible!

Scaffolded steps include ongoing, positive communication about school life between parent(s) and children and structured support for—but not interference with—learning at home. These steps in the scaffold can be visualized as moving parts—a need met in a certain way for one issue may need to be addressed in another way for a different issue.

It may be helpful to picture the scaffold in two ways: home-based involvement and school-based involvement. Home-based involvement includes how parents communicate with their adolescents about school issues and academic progress, including guidance with at-home learning and homework. School-based involvement includes the activities parents participate in at school, such as parent-teacher conferences and school events.

Home-Based Scaffolding

Home-based involvement includes high yet reasonable expectations of adolescents' abilities and aspirations. Students are significantly more likely to make steady academic progress when they are aware of their parents' high expectations. Consistent, positive, ongoing messages from parent to child result in enhanced self-esteem, interpersonal relatability, and improved self-perceptions of academic abilities.

What are high expectations? High expectations are your beliefs that your child *can* do well and *will* do well. Believe in your child, *tell* them often that you believe in them, give them examples of *why* you believe in them, and they will believe in themselves. But don't forget the scaffolds!

So what do scaffolds for high expectations look like, sound like, and feel like? High expectations are supportive, reasonable, and open-ended. Guide your child to pursue areas of interest and use their strengths to build their areas of potential growth. For example, if your child is strong in the visual arts, suggest overt connections to the math that they've found challenging. Creative problem-solving, strategic thinking, concept evaluation, and use of analysis to determine next-step decision-making occur in both areas of study. Highlighting these connections stimulates open-ended perspectives. Guided questions can facilitate this perspective:

- Can this math concept be visualized in a picture or 3D model?

- What math tools are also used in visual arts?

- How many small "mistakes" does a visual artist make in the process of completing a piece of art?

- If small errors are part of the artistic process, then aren't they part of the mathematical process, too?

Even small connections to areas of strength will provide foundational links to less accessible academic areas. The reasonable expectation that your teen can make these connections and grow in both areas sends a message to your child that you believe in their abilities and creative potential.

The application of high expectations includes the transfer of some decision-making from parent to adolescent through reflective, casual, ongoing discussions about educational goals and academic and social issues. At home and school, brief, supportive conversations build trusting relationships and improve overall student satisfaction, engagement, and achievement. These discussions can become a habit that feels comfortable. Don't be afraid to ask your child:

- What do you want for yourself out of ___ (math class, social connection, sport, part-time job)?

- What can you do to make that happen?

- How can I support you?

- Are there any obstacles you'll have to overcome?

- How could you overcome them?

- What are your aspirations for the end of the semester?

- Where do you picture yourself a year from now (in math, in the friendship, on the team, etc.)?

- What are the small and big steps you can take to make that happen?

- What resources would help you?

High expectations should be based on the assumption that the teen is the sculptor of their own success, provided they have parents who believe they can achieve (because then they will believe it themselves). High-expectation parents anticipate that their adolescents will take the lead with moderately challenging tasks.

Encouragement can be offered through scaffolded questioning:

- How do you think (the problem) could be solved?

- What strategies do you know?

- What resources could you use?

Parents can also extend themselves as sources of support:

- What might you need from me to be successful?

- Are there any obstacles in the way that I can help you with?

- Are there any opportunities that seem hard to access right now?

Adolescents will sometimes invite such support, but parents should also learn to wait to receive the invitation to do so.

Mentor Support

An additional and important question is: "Who is someone at school whom you trust and can go to for support, help, or advice?" Every child needs multiple sources of adult support—different issues, different adults—in order to successfully manage the many challenges of high school. In a new school setting, this question cannot be answered at the beginning of freshman year, but conveying the expectation that adults in the school are there to support your child will result in your child flagging those sources in their mind's eye, and, eventually, reaching out to them as needed.

Self-Efficacy

"Self-efficacy" can be described as an adolescent's level of confidence in their ability to exercise control over their motivations, behaviors, and the physical and social settings in which they interact. This confidence is built upon their prior experiences, their ability to visualize future success, observed experiences or the modeling of others, how they have experienced the sensations of their physical and emotional world, and the feedback they have received from guides or mentors. A child's self-efficacy is influenced by how parents convey their expectations and encourage autonomy while providing scaffolded levels of support.

Parents who effectively convey high expectations build the climate and conditions at home that foster the academic and social-emotional self-efficacy of their children. Supportive yet unobtrusive, these parents believe (and send messages that they believe) their children can problem-solve independently and advocate for themselves, and then allow them space to do so.

Physical Space and Resources

"Space" includes the physical space where your teen organizes their academic life at home, as well as the mental/emotional space involved in at-home decision-making about school-related tasks. Supportive physical spaces (visualized and created by your adolescent, with your input as needed) are where unobtrusive and flexible scaffolds exist, such as a comfortable work area (with available tools and adornments like notebooks, pens, and pillows), online or paper reference calendars with due dates, and subject-aligned resource lists. Resources might include email addresses for online teacher access; friends in classes who could answer homework questions; academic, subject-based reference terms; and online platforms. This scaffolded, home-based involvement creates an atmosphere that encourages self-sufficiency and open conversation about school and, more importantly, life.

Gradual Release of Responsibility

This process is mirrored in the teaching world as the **gradual release of responsibility**. For example, teachers engage in modeling *with* students to set the stage for how they interact within the classroom, organize the classroom space, and determine what kind of atmosphere they want to have and what kind of person they want to be while in that space. Routines, expectations, and how to access and use systems of support are discussed and modeled by teachers and practice-modeled by students to create a framework that leads to higher levels of emotional safety, comfort, and engagement. There are no assumptions and no surprises—expertise is built within a scaffolded and gradual release of responsibility model. With academic instruction, teachers model and students practice with frequent and constructive teacher feedback, often for extended periods of time, prior to being released to practice independently. Multiple opportunities for modeling and practice build strong habits that can be replicated with little effort. Scaffolds such as graphic organizers and access to multiple resources (i.e., math manipulatives, essay examples, online sources such as Khan Academy, or reference texts) are available for independent use. Students are encouraged to engage in conversation with peers and teachers, create their own strategies, and articulate for themselves what works and what doesn't, all within the embrace of a belief system of expected and anticipated success.

Whether it is parents providing home-based, scaffolded levels of support or teachers implementing a classroom-based gradual release of responsibility model, the goal is the same: autonomous, emotionally connected learners who are able to transfer their learning to new and gradually more complex concepts and tasks. By design, student self-efficacy is the bridge that leads to cognitive and creative achievement.

School-Based Scaffolding

School-based parental involvement includes parent-teacher conferences, participation in school events, and establishing discussions about scheduling choices and options for academic and social-emotional support. School-based involvement facilitates a team connection to home-based involvement strategies.

For example, some high schools offer monitored study halls ("monitored" as in staffed by a certified teacher). A parent of a math-anxious freshman might schedule a meeting to plan the child's schedule so that the certified staff member in the study hall is a math teacher, and instructional expertise is available to the student at that time. Or, if the adolescent has been identified as having ADHD and takes morning medication, the parent would reach out to the school to address the need to avoid a first-period math class. Conversations start between parent and child, and, as needed, the parent builds and assists in maintaining the bridge between school and home. School-based parental involvement increases the child's ability to adapt to the expectations within the school. The adolescent will gradually increase their ability to advocate for themselves and communicate clearly and frequently with teachers and parents.

Closing Advice

Scaffolded support involves being responsive to an adolescent's developmental, social-emotional, and academic needs while providing carefully structured steps in the process. Ask questions and listen without judgment to the responses. Pause before answering. *Believe* that your child wants the same things out of high school that you want *for* them: to feel a sense of connection and belonging, to make academic and social-emotional growth, and, by graduation, to become an independent, self-sufficient young adult ready to enter the world and embrace their future. Consistently high aspirations for your child, expressed often and combined with encouragement and support for learning, is significant to your adolescent's growth and achievement.

Chapter 3

CHOOSING CLASSES

A deep dive into course selection

Tiffany Richard
2012 Kansas State Teacher of the Year

I think of the difference between choosing classes in 8th versus 9th grades as the difference between choosing ice cream at McDonald's and Baskin-Robbins. McDonald's will give you a choice between vanilla and chocolate, but Baskin-Robbins has 31 flavors to choose from. While it's fun to choose among so many flavors, it can be overwhelming to decide as the line of other customers backs up behind you. In 9th grade, your student will still have the choice between advanced and regular level courses, but they will also have a whole new set of elective options to choose from. Each year of high school will add more options for students as they complete the required classes, just as Baskin-Robbins adds flavors of the month and makes seasonal flavor rotations. With all of these options, where do you start? How do you make the best choices?

One way to tackle these decisions is to follow author and management expert Stephen Covey's advice to begin with the end in mind. Ask your student to think ahead to their high school graduation.

- How do you want to feel when you walk across the graduation stage?

- What will a successful high school experience look like for you?

- Where do you see yourself going after graduation?

- If college, what career interests or majors are you considering?

- If technical, career, or military plans, what experiences do you need during high school to make that happen?

These questions should lead your student to think not only about the types of courses they are interested in, but also about the purpose of high school. Students often feel like school is being done to them instead of being for them. The more decisions students can make about their own courses, the more likely they are to feel in control of their goals. This can help students keep going when classes become difficult, not only because they made the choice to take these classes, but because they also have a purpose or goals that they are working toward. I had a student who struggled to remain on his chosen high school path, and we spent much time discussing his goals and what he needed to do to be successful in the present. He wrote out the quote, "Make your dreams bigger than your excuses," and used that to remind himself why he needed to continue working hard in all his classes. Were some of his classes still difficult? Yes. But with his purpose in mind, he shifted his mindset and took on the challenge. If your student is feeling stressed about their classes during the school year, this can be a good time to remind them of this discussion and the purpose of high school for them.

The Four-Year Plan

Unlike the previous grades that could stand alone, 9th- through 12th-grade courses add together to meet specific graduation requirements that are determined by your state and district. If your school offers a parent night for course selection, plan to attend with your student. Your school will also have a course planning guide or catalog that will list all of the requirements and course options. This guide may be on paper or online, and it will have short explanations for each course. Have your student spend time looking through these course options to find what courses interest or excite them. I suggest that you also look through the courses, but let your student lead the way in this discussion. This should be a fun time to consider all of the "flavors" your school has to offer. Remember, the more choices your students make for themselves, the more ownership they will take of their course selections. If you noticed a course that you think your student would enjoy but that they did not mention as a possibility, you may suggest that they look at the course description—but don't push them into a choice. This was a difficult area for me as a parent, especially because both of my children went to the high school where I taught. Because I knew my children and my school well, I wanted to create the perfect course plan for them. However, I had to remind myself many times that high school is for them, and they needed the ownership of making these choices. It is much better for them to realize that a course or path wasn't the best choice for them in high school, where they have a larger support system, than later in college or their career.

A great way to help your student make the best choices and feel ownership is to create a four-year course plan. This will help your student map out how and when they will be able to take the classes they are most excited about. This will help your student avoid being in junior year and realizing they have run out of time to take some courses they wanted to. Many schools have an online four-year planning program or a page in the course planning guide to use as a template. I suggest having your student create their four-year plan electronically and update it each year. If the school doesn't have an online version, then you can create a spreadsheet or table on the computer for each year of high school. Use the course planning guide to input the required classes for each year. For example, core classes (math, science, English, social studies) usually have a sequential path with three to four years of required courses. Prerequisites are usually needed for advanced courses. For example, your student may be excited to take a forensic science class but may not have selected a chemistry course—although chemistry is a required prerequisite. Knowing prerequisites will guide your students' chosen science path.

Your district will also have requirements for the number of courses within each elective area. Creating a four-year plan to ensure all the requirements will be covered, along with the chosen electives, is important. For example, many schools require two years of an international language. If your student took Spanish in 8th grade, then it might be best to continue Spanish in 9th and 10th grades, or they may want to try a new language.

This is also a good time to look at requirements outside of graduation. If your student is considering college, look at entrance requirements for your state or colleges of interest. This can also help guide your student through course selection.

Advanced Class Choices

Parents also can help students decide whether or not to take advanced classes. If a student wants the academic distinction of graduating in the top 10%, it's important to understand the school's grading system. Advanced classes usually have a higher weight in the GPA calculation. If your teen is a highly successful academic student and wants to work toward this tier, then it's important to ensure that enough weighted classes are taken to achieve the highest GPA possible. This can be highly competitive, so it should only be encouraged for students who are not just strong academically, but who also have strong study and time-management skills. Advanced classes will require a larger study time commitment and increased stress for the student, so they should be chosen with care.

Why Advanced Classes?

As a science instructional coach, I have the opportunity to work with students at all levels. One student asked to move out of his pre-AP (Advanced Placement) chemistry class because it was just too hard and too much work. I began by asking about his purpose for being in an advanced class, and he said that this was the class his previous teacher put him in. I realized that he didn't understand the purpose of taking advanced classes, so when the class "got hard," he didn't see a reason to work harder because he could just drop down to the regular level.

Here are some of the reasons for staying in the harder class that I shared with him:

1. You can earn college credit, either by passing the AP exam, passing a dual college credit class, or completing the International Baccalaureate program.

2. The number of credits you can obtain in high school varies, but many students can begin college as a second-semester freshman or even a sophomore, which lets them graduate early and save money. This may also allow you to take a smaller class load in college, which is helpful if you are taking a difficult course.

3. According to the College Board, students who take one or more AP exams are more likely to graduate from college within four years. This is most likely due to the increase in study skills and

higher-level thinking that these advanced classes provide. My students in the Advancement Via Individual Determination (AVID) college prep program have reported that college was easier than they thought it would be. AVID helped students not previously on a college track to prepare for at least one college prep class per semester. When in college, they said their friends who did not take advanced classes were having a more difficult time learning the study and time-management skills needed for college success.

How Many Advanced Classes?

Most schools offer many choices for advanced classes, such as AP Art and AP Music. Look through the school's course offerings with your student, and determine where they have the most interest. Most core classes (math, science, English, social studies) have an advanced option. Your student's current teacher most likely recommended the course they feel your student is ready for. See if your student agrees with this recommendation. Also, ask your student these questions: Are you prepared for the challenge and extra time an advanced class will require? Do you have other after-school time needs or responsibilities? Do you want to enroll in all advanced classes, or are there one or two you'd like to start with?

Being Realistic

Knowing when to push your student or hold them back is always tricky. We want our students to get the most out of their school experience, but we also don't want them to be overly stressed or even unsuccessful by biting off more than they can chew. Freshmen tend to live in the moment and judge themselves harshly in comparison to their peers. Remind your student that changes or adjustments can always be made. They are not "stupid" if they don't take advanced classes as freshmen; they are "smart" for making the best choices for themselves.

This is where the four-year plan can be valuable. If your student is worried about the transition to high school, then 9th grade could be a year for focusing on the basics and finding their interests. The four-year plan can include advanced classes starting in sophomore year. Many students I've worked with have been able to add advanced classes after freshman year with success because they had the plan in place and knew that they were working toward increasing study skills for movement into advanced classes.

Changing Course

Once the school year is underway, your student may struggle in one or more advanced classes. Remind your student that it's not the end of the world. Reach out to the teacher for information on where they think that struggle is occurring. Ask the teacher:

- Is it more of an issue with the content level or with study skills?
- How can your student improve in the course?
- Should the student stay in the advanced course or move to the regular course?

Ask your student:

- Where are you struggling in this class? Is it classroom work? The study time commitment? Testing?
- What ideas do you have to increase your success?
- Have you noticed other students who are successful and what they are doing? Is there anyone you could study with?
- Do you think that moving to the regular level course would allow you to work on your study skills, so that you could move into the advanced course in the next year or two?

Special Education

If your student is in special education, much of the planning of high school classes will be aided by the Individualized Education Program developed for your student and by the special education teacher, who is responsible for the IEP. The team that wrote your student's IEP will meet with you yearly, and you might investigate course offerings before your last middle school meeting prior to high school. The team's goal will be to place the student in the regular classroom as much of the day as possible, but there may be courses they take within the special education department. You need to know the goals the team will work toward in each classroom and how they will be evaluated.

The IEP committee will have determined what is needed to help your student successfully complete core curriculum and will discuss any modifications or accommodations that might be necessary for your student's success. If the course is being modified, your student may be allowed more time to take a test, or they may have someone read test questions to them. If the student is accommodated, they may not be required to learn all the material. The student may, for instance, be required to recognize and correctly label landforms, but the student may not have to explain the differences between landforms like other students will be required to do.

In addition to the core curriculum, your student will have electives to choose from. Does your student like art? Building things? Cooking? Look at the catalog together, and talk about what they would like to explore.

Although your student will have a special education teacher to check on their progress, you should also check in with both their regular teacher and special education teacher to make sure your student stays on track.

Electivos

All schools will require a certain number of credits within each elective area. Depending on the size of your school, there will be various offerings. This is an area where students can have fun and try different options. And just because these courses are not considered core classes does not mean they are not valuable. Sometimes it is the elective class that motivates a student to keep coming to school. This is where students may discover a passion outside of core academic work, and these classes can teach important life skills.

I still have a clay pot that one of my students made as a freshman. He was upset by how it had turned out and wanted to throw it away, so I asked to display it in my biology classroom. We discussed how his work would improve over time and how his skills would continue to develop. He stuck with pottery, and his skills definitely improved. When I visited his house for his graduation party, he had many beautiful pottery items on display. I joked about having the "best" of all of his pottery work, and he offered to give me one of his beautiful senior year products. I was honored to keep his original, and I use it as an example for my biology students to show that all learning requires practice, and the expectation is never perfection on the first, or even fourth, attempt. That perseverance learned in elective classes can be related to core academic classes.

This is an area where students can try out different occupations as well. I had a student who was sure she wanted to follow in her father's path and work in business. After taking two different business classes, she realized that she did not enjoy business at all. At first, she was upset that she didn't like her chosen area, but we talked through the benefit of her realizing this in high school versus later, in college. She then realized that her love for her cooking class could result in a culinary career. She is now happily working as a sous chef, and she is thankful that she discovered this path during high school exploration.

Many of our highly driven academic students do not see the usefulness of elective courses, but these can be valuable opportunities for student stress relief. Students who are active tend to perform better cognitively, so athletics and PE classes can give students a boost in their day. My daughter was determined to achieve at the highest level and didn't see a need for an elective class such as art. However, she enrolled in photography, completed an AP art class, and discovered a passion for this medium. Even though she received a STEM scholarship and completed a biochemistry degree, her art experience served her well, because she also received an art scholarship and discovered that art was invaluable for managing stress and anxiety during college. She now has a creative outlet she can turn to throughout life.

Ask:

- Which electives are you interested in?
- Have you considered [insert course you think your student would enjoy]?

Career and Technical Courses

Most school districts offer opportunities for technical or skilled labor training and certifications. While these opportunities are usually offered in the upper grades, it's good to keep those options in mind when selecting courses now. If your student is interested in taking these courses, they need to make sure they have completed enough of the required courses during the first two years in order to qualify. Not only do these classes offer opportunities for jobs after high school, but they also often provide experience in a career field. I had a student who wanted to complete a four-year degree but who loved cars. He took an auto mechanics course where he not only received a certification to work in that area, but he also found his career path. He worked part-time as an auto mechanic throughout college and completed a mechanical engineering degree. With his experience and degree, he was hired to work in design in the auto industry. Without this experience, he would not have been as readily hired, and he would not have had the higher-salaried part-time job throughout college. Other students have benefited from getting their certified nursing assistant or emergency medical technician certification during high school. This gives students an opportunity to try out the field to see if they enjoy it, while also gaining valuable experience.

Military

If your student is interested in joining the military, they will not only need to complete their high school diploma, but they will also take a military readiness test called the Advanced Services Vocational Aptitude Battery (ASVAB). This test is used to help military branches determine which vocational area and jobs are best for each recruit. It's beneficial to take high school classes seriously and make sure that basic skills are strong. If your school doesn't have a JROTC program, the recruiting office may have programs to help students prepare physically for the military. Your student can use their school's PE offerings, such as weight training, to prepare for boot camp.

Extracurriculars

This may not seem to fit into a section on course selections; however, planning time for extracurriculars does go along with planning a student's course load. Although "extra" curricular implies that this is a course outside of the daily curriculum, there is often a period during the school day for these options. If a student is involved in athletics, for example, that may include a course during the school day as well as practices and games outside the school day. Performing arts, such as theater and band, are often courses held during the day, although rehearsals and practices after school will also be required.

If your student is not already planning for an extracurricular activity, encourage them to explore their options. As other chapters will discuss, being involved in school is beneficial for a student's success, not just academically but socially and emotionally as well. For college-bound students looking for scholarships or entrance into competitive universities, showing involvement outside the classroom is expected. Students should try out different clubs and organizations within their school as 9th graders and see where they fit best. Organizations and clubs can give students not just opportunities to meet and work with a variety of other students, but also opportunities for leadership roles. Leadership not only develops a student's skill set, but it also is something many scholarship committees look for. Ask:

- What activities are you interested in participating in at school?
- What clubs or organizations do you want to try out?
- What volunteer opportunities are you interested in?
- If in athletics, a performing art, or other activity that is scheduled daily, how do you plan to schedule time for after-school requirements?

Work

Most freshmen will not have an outside job, but they will begin thinking about how they can make some extra money. Work experience can be valuable for students, but it can also impact the time they have for their academic work and extracurricular activities. When creating the four-year plan, take into account whether your student will be looking for an outside job and include that in the planning. For example, if your student wants to have a job during the 11th-grade year to save up for a car, then they need to consider how many advanced classes and extracurricular activities they can be involved in and still be successful in school.

Closing Advice

Exploring course selection options is a time for students to start making decisions for themselves, which gives parents the opportunity to become partners in their learning. The key to course selection is to plan for change. Between 9th and 12th grades, an amazing amount of growth occurs. Allow your student the flexibility to change course plans and to take on new challenges as they grow and learn more about themselves. Many of tomorrow's careers have not even been created. Allowing your student to learn how to use their skills and interests to guide them will help them develop that important mindset so that they can be successful in our ever-changing world.

Chapter 4
A SENSE OF BELONGING

How students can make connections at school

Heidi Crumrine
2018 New Hampshire State Teacher of the Year

It is a very strange feeling dropping off your child for their first day of high school. Memories of your own time in high school come flooding back, and you can't believe that this nearly-adult-looking person, who seemingly just moments ago was tightly strapped in a car seat, is now walking into high school. Just as when they started kindergarten, our minds fill with questions and worry. *Will the other kids be nice? Will they make friends? Will they have someone to sit with at lunch? What if they need me and I'm not there?* We have so much hope in our hearts as they step through those front doors.

It's All About Connection

We all know what it is like to belong. It is an almost overwhelming feeling that makes everything else in life feel manageable. The joy that comes with feeling like you are safe, comfortable in your environment, and surrounded by people with whom you connect can help you feel like you can overcome nearly any obstacle. This feeling of connection and sense of purpose is what we hope for all of our children as they enter high school.

As a parent of a 9th grader myself, I am living this reality. To add another layer of complexity, she is a student at the high school where I teach. I love it; she's still not so sure about it. I have watched her turn away from me when she has spotted me in the hall, throw her head into her hands when she realized I was coming into her English class in my role as a literary coach, and, of course, come to me for money or snacks when she needs something. Luckily for you and your child, you will probably have more space during your day than we do.

I have taught 9th grade for nearly 20 years and, while much has changed during this time, what has not is a desire for connection and community that is at the core of the high school experience. This sense of connection and community is not just about being prom queen or making the varsity soccer team. According to the American Psychological Association, students who feel connected to their school communities perform better academically, have better school attendance, and stay in school longer. In short, feeling connected to school is of foundational importance to a young person's success in high school, and 9th grade is the year where that can begin to happen.

Facilitating Connections

It can feel challenging to help a young person transition from middle school to high school because there is so much that is new: a new building, new students, new school culture, new teachers, and new routines, to name a few. Complicating matters is the fact that most 14-year-olds don't want their parents anywhere near them when this transition is happening. We all know the importance of having friends, but we can't simply arrange a playdate with a mutual friend to help facilitate a friendship. You can't force your child to join a team or club, and you can't drop them off at the Saturday night football game and say, "Have fun! Make some friends!"

How should a parent support a child as they transition into high school so that the teen has agency in forming their identity, while also nudging the teen along when they are reluctant to engage? While it certainly seems like there are a lot of things a parent cannot do, there are many that you can. It's not easy, but, luckily, any good high school will have lots of pathways for students to explore and a building full of adults who know how to support them as they do that.

Many high schools offer summer programming for incoming freshmen. This is often in the form of orientation-style activities, and it is a perfect opportunity for your child to get connected to school before the year even starts. Attending orientation allows a student to interact with staff members in a low-key environment, practice getting around the building, and connect with some new students. Whether or not any of these interactions result in lifelong friendships or inspiration is irrelevant. What it does is get your child into the building to practice connecting with others in ways that can lead to greater success in 9th grade and beyond.

Extracurricular Connections

Below are some other pathways where your student can make connections as they enter their first year of high school.

Athletics

Joining a fall sports team is an easy way to fast-track a connection to a new school. It is convenient when your child is excited about a sport that takes place during the fall, because there are normally preseason practices, which means an athlete can begin to feel connected to and engaged in their school before the school year even begins. In the years that I have taught 9th grade, I have observed that my students who are engaged in a fall sports activity transition much more quickly to the high school experience. They have a sense of investment in their campus, and they have made connections with students across all grade levels before school has even started.

That said, participation in a fall sport is not a requirement for social engagement in high school. Any participation on a sports team, regardless of time of year, allows a student to be engaged with and connected to their school community beyond academics. Ask the school:

- Do you have any no-cut sports?
- Do you offer Unified Sports? How do we sign up?
- Can a student have a nonathletic supporting role, such as an equipment manager?

Performing Arts

The beauty of performing arts opportunities for students in high school is that there are so many different roles for so many different kinds of students, whether in music or through acting. Performing arts students are often also athletes, volunteers, or school leaders, so they are a great group of students to connect with because they can help connect your student to other facets of the school. In addition to performing on stage, students can work on set design or lighting; manage backstage, costumes, and community relations; or direct. I have never met a performing arts group that turned away a volunteer or someone who was interested in supporting the program. I have found the performing arts departments to be inclusive, welcoming, and enthusiastic about students being involved. Ask the school:

- Can a student join the band, orchestra, or chorus with no previous experience?

- What are the supporting roles available for students in performing arts?

- Is there somewhere that students can come to practice their instruments and connect with other performing arts students?

Clubs and Leadership

While athletics and performing arts groups are often structured programs integrated into the school day or school system, they are not the only ways for a student to become involved in their school community. A club can offer more scheduling flexibility than athletics or performing arts. Furthermore, most schools allow students to create a club based on a common interest as long as it can find an advisor. At my high school, there have been clubs for surfing (I live in central New Hampshire), feminism, United Nations, and fishing. All have been student-driven. Some have lasted a few years and fizzled out, and others have continued despite changes in student interest. The point is, if your child is interested in exploring a particular area of interest, it is likely that someone at their school will be willing to help them create a club or organization to support it.

High schools also have leadership roles that are often a combination of election-driven and volunteer-driven programming. While your student may not be elected class president, they can still attend leadership meetings and serve as a liaison to their peers. If a student is interested in pursuing a leadership role, they might simply need to ask who needs help and how to get involved. Ask the school:

- How do students learn about clubs offered at school?

- How does a student create their own club and find an advisor?

- Can parents advise student clubs?

Teacher and Staff Connections

While a teenager's social life revolves around friendships, connection with adults still carries significant weight. According to the Association for Supervision and Curriculum Development, research consistently indicates that students who are connected to an adult in their school are more engaged and thus better able to succeed. If your child has a teacher who they gravitate toward, don't hesitate to reach out to that teacher to let them know. You are not suggesting that this person do extra work to engage with your child, but if a teacher knows that a student feels safe with and connected to them, it gives them insight that they might not recognize. Encourage your child to open up to staff members and allow yourself to be okay with the fact that you aren't in control of every connection your child makes.

Insight from 9th Graders

I asked students what advice they had for incoming freshmen about how getting involved helped them, and this is what they said:

- "Being in a sport was really good for me in the fall, because even though I wasn't friends with any upperclassmen, I knew faces at school. It's like I was taking it in smaller steps as I transitioned to high school."

- "Being in activities makes me less introverted because it makes me talk with different and more people."

- "Being involved in activities helped me get to know people. I'm glad I did it early in the year because it just made everything easier."

When It's Not Going Well

The reality is, no matter what, your child will struggle with feeling connected at some point in high school. For some students this will be a bigger challenge than others, but it is not something that anyone can avoid. And that's okay.

A successful transition to high school doesn't mean being involved in and taking advantage of *every* opportunity that presents itself. A growing body of research is indicating that students who are hyper-scheduled have higher incidences of anxiety, depression, and burnout. The goal of high school is be involved in ways that matter and feel manageable to your child and that bring joy and a sense of connection.

Closing Advice

Transitioning to high school is a big adjustment, regardless of where a student attended middle school. That transition is not just significant for the student, but it is significant for parents, as well. However, armed with knowledge about the programming provided by your school, an understanding of your child, and a willingness to engage with your school, that transition can be made smoother. And it is just a small moment in time for your child as they grow into adulthood.

Conversation Starters

- Who is an adult in the building with whom you can connect to ask questions?

- Who do you tend to hang around with at lunch?

- What do you do when you're feeling alone?

- Tell me about a time when you felt connected to your school community.

- How do you solve a problem when you are in school?

Chapter 5

HOW CAN I HELP MY STUDENT SUCCEED IN THE CLASSROOM?

Tips on building executive function

Mandy Manning
2018 National and Washington State
Teacher of the Year

In March 2020, when the COVID-19 pandemic shut down schools across the United States, educators and parents had the opportunity to reflect on the difficulties students faced as they attempted to engage in learning outside of a classroom. One glaring reality was the need to focus on the skills we develop through **executive functioning**.

Executive function encompasses mental processing, organization, and planning. These include skills such as working memory, flexible thinking, and impulse control. As students transition to a more independent learning environment, their executive functioning skills become even more of a necessity, especially during the transition from middle school to high school.

As a 21-year veteran teacher with significant experience teaching 9th-grade students, I've witnessed the changes that students encounter as they are required to become more independent. They need support in applying the skills they have been learning since they were in preschool, such as organization, time management, self-control, and using their working memory to move from one task to the next and one classroom to another.

As a parent, I also experienced this transition in my own home as my son and daughter navigated the change from elementary to middle school, then middle to high school, then from in-class to remote learning. I found, at each stage, as a parent with the lens of a teacher, that my role was to support the development of my children's executive functioning skills.

My daughter had significant organizational skills, was intrinsically motivated, and weathered each experience easily. My son, on the other hand, struggled with remembering his schedule and assignments, planning his day, and keeping his work organized. As I puzzled through how to support his learning during the pandemic, I was reminded of every transition he had gone through and the supports he needed to be successful through each new challenge.

One of the heaviest lifts for our children is the shift from middle school to high school. While grades are important in middle school, they are not part of your student's permanent record. In high school, however, grades are vital. Grades determine whether students pass to the next level, impact college admissions, and, whether fairly or not, tell a story about a child's academic abilities. Ninth grade is an imperative year and sets the stage for the remainder of high school.

As parents, we have the desire to protect and shield our children from challenges. We want their pathway to be easy, with few obstacles. Sometimes we overcompensate, taking care of things and clearing their path to the detriment of their independence and growth. Our role should be more of a guide. We should not do for them, but support them and empower them to do for themselves. Below are some ways to support your child's classroom success.

Building Intrinsic Motivation

Because of the internet and cell phones, young people are used to instant gratification. All information is at their fingertips, and they have grown accustomed to not having to wait. School is a long game and as kids move into upper grades, class periods are longer, coursework builds from one level to the next, and it can be difficult to focus on a finish line that is still a few years away. Students need to understand and practice delayed gratification. Help your teen set **short-term goals**, such as completing a project by a due date, and **long-term goals**, like finishing the first semester of 9th grade with an 80 average or better in each class. Then, help them mark each step and celebrate each movement forward. A practical way to do this is to keep a calendar and mark the days or the tasks toward the end goal. Start a vision board to help your child visualize their ultimate goal of graduating, moving on to higher education or getting a job, or something equally meaningful. Most importantly, the goal must be your student's. *They* have to be excited to get there. That may mean that their goal does not exactly line up with the goals you would like them to achieve. The key is to support them in realizing *their* dreams.

Another way to build intrinsic motivation is to help your child understand **the relevance** of what they are learning in school to their future goals. The more your child can connect what they are learning in school to what they are doing in their daily lives, the more they will focus on and care about school and their classwork. Sometimes it can be difficult to make these connections. You may have to solicit the help of one of your child's teachers to help both of you recognize these connections. Relevance to life is important, but so is relevance to passion. Once in high school, every class your child takes is a stepping stone. Help your child plan their school schedule according to what they want to achieve. Make sure they've connected with their school counselor to ensure the classes they are taking are the right ones for them, as well as the classes they need to graduate on time.

Helping with Homework

Helping your child with homework can be very difficult at this stage in their schooling, as we do not always have the skills or knowledge to do so. One way to overcome this obstacle is to engage your child's peers through **study groups** and **organized collaboration**. Peers are important to your child. As kids grow, their friends take precedence in their lives. Become the home where kids come together to do their homework and work on projects. You'll be helping your child and also their friends. If your home is not the ideal setting, help your child organize a place they can go to collaborate, like the library or a coffee shop. The key is to create routines that help them complete their work in a supportive and engaging environment.

Another way to help your child with their homework is to help them prioritize and organize their assignments. Teach them how to effectively use **an agenda** to keep track of their classes, assignments, and due dates. Check their agenda regularly, and ask them about their assignments. This will help them verbalize the expectations of the assignment. If they cannot verbalize the expectations, help them to locate the directions, and, if they still lack understanding, remind them to ask their teachers for clarification.

Reinforce skills for searching the internet for pertinent and factual information—not copying and pasting—writing what they learn in their own words while citing the source of that information. Encourage your child to proofread, edit, and check their assignments to ensure that they have addressed everything that was expected of them. Finally, resist doing your child's work for them. Even when a project or an assignment is difficult, it is essential that they do the work on their own.

Developing Study Skills

In addition to helping your child organize their homework, encourage good study skills. The first step is organization and planning. When my son nearly did not pass his classes after remote learning began, I realized he needed more structure. When his teachers were no longer there to provide reminders, he didn't know what to do. We set up a big calendar at his study station and taught him how to keep track of due dates and upcoming assessments and then to create a **study plan**. A study plan should include what and how to study, as well as specific timelines. Reviewing notes daily and answering practice questions each day does so much more for working memory and recall than trying to study everything just before an exam. Keeping the calendar develops time-management skills and helps kids prioritize their work, while also leaving room for social and personal activities. The study station is also important. It should be organized and phone- and distraction-free and have everything your child needs to prioritize their work, whether that's a computer or a clear place where they can comfortably have their book and notebook open.

One critical study habit is **positive self-talk**. Studying can be daunting, especially when a child is not yet confident in the subject or skill they are learning. Just like we do as adults, our children also experience regular and frightening crises of confidence. Help your child come up with a mantra, or saying, they can repeat when they are not feeling confident or have lost focus. It can be something simple— "I am capable, I can learn"—or more goal-focused—"I want to own my own business, so math is important to my life, and I want to learn this." Your child may need support to work through academic and social issues. Encourage them to keep a journal, because writing through their challenges can help them clear their minds in order to focus on their schoolwork.

Responding if Your Child Falls Behind or Encounters Learning Challenges

Watching your child struggle in school is always difficult. I have watched kids struggle for all sorts of reasons. Sometimes it's as simple as being disorganized and losing their work or forgetting to turn things in. Many of the strategies I have addressed above, such as support in organization and planning, can solve these situations. At times, though, students have actual learning challenges, whether from a diagnosed learning issue such as ADD or dyslexia, or from one that has not yet been diagnosed, like a processing issue that makes it difficult for a child to follow directions. These types of challenges require more attention.

First and foremost, it is essential to support your child in becoming a **self-advocate**. The first part of self-advocacy is developing skills in impulse control and organization. Once your child has the organizational and planning skills to keep track of their schedule, learning, and work expectations, they need support in speaking up for themselves. Help your child be confident in approaching their teachers about their progress and any assistance they need to complete their assignments or understand what is expected of them. We sometimes want to talk to a teacher ourselves, but it is important to let your child speak to the teacher first. If you do have to talk to the teacher about a problem, go into the conversation with curiosity, seeking not to solve the problem but to understand it better to help *your child* solve the problem.

Second, if your child is falling behind because of learning challenges, look on the surface first to determine the scaffolds (see chapter 2 for more on scaffolding support) your child may need. These scaffolds are supports I've already discussed, such as keeping an agenda and prioritizing work. If the problem is deeper and no amount of scaffolding seems to help, work with your child's teacher to determine if there is a possible learning delay. Seek assessment, and then work with your child's teacher to determine available classroom- and school-level supports, as well as any additional outside resources, such as tutoring, that you can access to get your child the help they need to be successful in the classroom.

Being Present and Interested

The most important thing that parents can do in supporting classroom success is to be present and interested. When your child knows that you care about what they are doing inz school, their learning experiences, and their performance, they are more likely to care themselves and put forth effort. Being present and interested means sharing your own stories about school, the challenges and the successes, and being completely honest. Ask your child what they did at school, what brought them joy, what was a challenge, and what they still need to accomplish. Check up on them and make it a routine that they are used to, one that requires more than a one- or two-word answer. Above all, when they answer, respond with interest and wonder, not judgment or unsolicited advice. As children grow into adolescents, we can only give them the tools they need, not force them to use those tools.

Closing Advice

Our role as parents is to provide guidance through unconditional love. As our children get older, our participation in their lives lessens more and more. We volunteer less at their schools, and we go to fewer functions. We gradually release our responsibility and empower them to be independent humans who know how to take care of themselves and navigate the world around them. We give them the tools and the confidence to meet every challenge. They will fail. That's okay. The key is to help them learn from their failures and move forward more knowledgeable, capable, and brave.

Conversation Starters

- What are the major dates we need to remember for the first month of school? The first quarter? First semester? (Ask again at the start of second semester and as often as needed.)

- What are you doing in your classes this week? OR What did you do in your classes today?

- How are you organizing your assignments? What is most important to accomplish first?

- What do you want to have time to do this week that is not connected to your classes? How will you fit that into your class and homework schedule?

- What is your goal once you finish high school? What small goal can you make right now as a first step?

Chapter 6

OVERCOMING PROCRASTINATION AND RESETTING MOTIVATION

Strategies to support your student
in class and at home

Al Rabanera
Algebra Teacher, California

Pat was a quiet and easygoing student. There was a sense of calmness in the way he carried himself, as he was cautious to engage with other students. It was understandable, because it was his first time at a new school. Each day, as I stood in the doorway greeting and checking in with students, Pat would shuffle past me into the classroom with either a simple head nod or a "'sup." Some days, Pat would slouch in his chair, copying notes while tapping his pencil on the desk. Other days, he was alert, sitting up in his seat, asking questions. It would take a bit of time for us to develop a rapport and for Pat to open up.

I could tell that Pat was raised to be respectful by the way he behaved and by his effort and participation in class activities. He followed class rules and engaged regularly. However, at times his work production and the number of assignments submitted correctly and completely was low. He sometimes questioned when we would be using the skills learned in class in real life and why what we were learning was important. I think these questions were his way of covering for insecurities and learning gaps. As his challenges and struggles with grasping concepts began to increase, he started to think that his grades were a reflection of who he was. But that was so far from the truth. Pat's demeanor during class led me to believe that his insecurity with the grasp of problem skills and abilities led to being easily distracted in class. In other words, when the content became challenging, his attention would begin to drift, creating a lack of motivation and confidence to fully engage with the class.

Overcoming Procrastination

As Pat and I developed a rapport and he began to open up, I started to see who he was as a learner. Pat shared that he felt there were better things to spend his time on at home rather than working through the classroom content. I knew Pat was capable of completing the work and being successful in class, but he needed some self-monitoring strategies. Pat said that he felt he was not good at learning and that it would be easier to not try rather than to struggle and get the problems wrong. I knew that I could create the conditions for Pat, as well as his classmates, to thrive academically. I needed to provide opportunities for my students to experience small wins to build up their confidence, and teach them strategies to persevere through a productive struggle. Here are a few tips and tricks I use in the classroom that you can use at home to help your student mitigate their procrastination.

Be Specific and Intentional

Pat would benefit from clear and concise communication, the key to student learning and achievement. By setting clear and high expectations for students, I provided the structure that Pat wanted and needed to be successful in learning the content. I also created, with my students, **classroom norms** that, in turn, lowered Pat's affective filters (which block cognition) by providing predictability. These classroom norms (i.e., be on time, come prepared, be respectful toward your peers and teacher, bring only positive energy to the classroom) help my community of learners to thrive by making the classroom expectations we have for each other clear.

At home, let your student know what the high expectations you are setting for them and for yourself are. An example would be creating and modeling how to use an agenda to prioritize activities, set goals, and celebrate achievements. You need to be invested in the success of your student. Be explicit, because what you may imply about your high expectations may not always be interpreted the same way by your student. Be vocal about what you expect, and let them know how you are going to support them in meeting their goals. Create a space for your student to study and complete homework assignments. Make sure that the tools, resources, and support that your student needs are easily accessible.

Redirect Attention

When Pat procrastinated on assignments, his attention would typically begin to drift from the lesson to another activity that he believed was more interesting, ranging from daydreaming and drawing to talking to classmates and playing games on his cell phone. To bring Pat's attention back to the lesson, two of the most effective teaching strategies that I used were proximity and checking for understanding throughout the lesson. With the proximity instructional strategy, I reduced the physical distance between myself and Pat as a nonverbal way to communicate and redirect his attention. Checking in with Pat early and often gave him opportunities to practice verbalizing his understanding of the content and directing his attention back to the lesson.

At home, you could use proximity to monitor your student's use of social media and direct their attention back to completing assignments, which might help mitigate procrastination. Social media has become an addiction for students and adults alike. Monitoring, limiting, or even eliminating the time your student can access social media can be a powerful way to redirect your student's attention. On the flip side, providing access could also be leveraged into a reward system for completing assignments in a timely fashion. Checking in with your student is a little more challenging if you are not familiar with the academic content, but one easy way to do this is to have your student explain what the question is asking, what their answer is, and why they chose to answer the question or problem that way.

Be Encouraging and Create Value

At the beginning of each class, I review the daily agenda with my students. As part of the agenda, we review the learning objectives, the unit pacing, the schedule for the week, and how the lesson from yesterday connects to the content we are about to learn and how tomorrow's lesson builds from what I will teach today. By explaining to my students what we are going to be engaging with for the day, I create conditions for them to thrive. By encouraging my students and providing feedback on their progress, I am able to connect with them.

What would this look and sound like at home? When I was growing up, I was always encouraged to try my best, and if I tried my best, there was nothing more that could be expected of me. If you adopt this approach, the accountability shifts away from you and to your student. As I continued to grow as an educator, that same idea was called a **growth mindset**. A growth mindset will lead your student to believe that their skills can improve over time. Ask your student, "Are you trying your best?", and wait for their response. I recommend sharing your perspective about the importance of being able to work through procrastination and providing personal, relatable examples.

Motivation

To motivate Pat to refocus on the lesson and to complete assignments when he was in a slump, we had a conversation and focused on his "why." Our dialogue was framed around the ideas of *why* it was important for him to start an assignment early and to complete the assignment correctly, *why* it was important to stay on task, and *why* it was important to remain focused. Motivation is the process used to initiate, guide, and maintain goal-oriented behaviors, and I tie these ideas into personal accountability.

How to Create Awareness

When students get into a slump because of procrastination, often they will tell me they will finish the work at home and that they "already know how to do it." To help prevent falling behind on assignments, I have my students review their grades and assignments at the beginning of each week. I am providing my students an opportunity to review their progress, ask questions about assignments in which they did not earn full points, and see which assignments are missing. While my students are reviewing their grades, it gives me time to briefly check in with each of them to ask about their progress, encourage them, and find out how I can provide support for parts of the lessons or concepts with which they may be struggling.

At home, it is important for you to be just as aware as your student about their academic progress. If your student's grades are available online, I would recommend regularly checking them together to create an ongoing dialogue about their progress and how you can support them. You could also reach out to the teacher to ask specific questions about your student's effort and work habits, because they may have more context about your student's grades. You may also be able to provide the teacher with information that could help them provide strategies to better support your student's learning and academic achievement.

Creating and Implementing an Action Plan

"To fail to prepare is to prepare to fail."—Benjamin Franklin

Once Pat and I established the fact that he had been procrastinating, we had a conversation about how we could get him back on track. We started by discussing his goals for the class and how they matched the goals I had for him. This is important so that we are on the same page about how to move forward. We set up a plan and reviewed where he was. We talked about effort and work habits, not only for success in my class, but also so he could be a successful learner at school. These planning skills could be transferred to other classes and even be used outside the classroom to help Pat reach his goals.

At home, if you notice that your student is starting to fall behind, have a conversation to hear their perspective on what is going on with the class. Ask your student questions about how they think they can catch up and what their plan is to do so (see Conversation Starters below). I would recommend having your student email the teacher with their proposed plan, and copy you, so you can work together to mitigate the procrastination. With an action plan in place, the next steps would be to set it in motion and monitor its progress.

Closing Advice

When students are struggling to understand class content, they tend to procrastinate starting and completing their assignments. Being clear about your expectations and setting up a good workspace provides a strong foundation for them at home. Next, redirect their attention by checking in with them about their grades and social media use. Ask them *why* they may be procrastinating. Encourage them to try their best. Finally, help them create an action plan and communicate and set that plan in motion with their teacher.

Overcoming procrastination and resetting motivation can seem like a monstrous task. Be patient, because the process takes time to establish, build, and practice. Just like in teaching, breaking down each of these tasks into smaller activities and consistent practices can help reset a student's motivation.

Conversation Starters

- Can you name a subject or two in which you feel you are falling behind?

- How do you think you can catch up; what is your plan to do so?

- Why do you think students procrastinate when they feel unsure of an assignment?

- How do you think grades reflect who you are as a student?

- Can you tell me what you think my expectations are from you as a student (i.e., GPA)?

- How can I help you set up a good workspace at home?

- Which of your teachers starts class by setting an agenda? Do you find it helpful?

- In which classes do you think you are not trying your best? Why is this?

Chapter 7

OVERCOMING ACADEMIC SETBACKS

How to transform failures into opportunities

Bethany Bernasconi
2012 New Hampshire State Teacher of the Year

As soon as they walk in the door, you know something is up. Something seems off, just not right, and their typical after-school rituals are different than they've been every other day. It's that sinking feeling that something happened at school today, and it is time to figure out just what.

Lots of us have experienced this moment as parents. And in that moment, we have so many choices about how to process the information. All the initial questions, conversations, and approaches that likely spring to mind are really dependent on the relationship that you have with your child. The story might come out in a rush, over hours, or even over days. If the trouble is academic in nature, you have an opportunity to help your 9th grader shift their negative feelings into an opportunity for growth, to build resilience, strengthen teacher-student-family partnerships, and hone the skills that will support our teens as stronger students and young adults.

At certain moments in a student's academic career, there are greater leaps in maturity than others. There is consensus with teachers I've spoken with that the transitions from 4th to 5th, 8th to 9th, and 10th to 11th grades are true milestone moments when we are struck by how much students have grown when they return in the fall. As they transition into 9th grade, there seems to be a shift in the desire to be more independent and take greater ownership of their learning, which can sometimes leave parents feeling left out or not needed. Actually, the opposite is true, and parents can help determine the best approach to support their kids in a way that honors their continued development, allows for greater decision-making on their part, and models the skills like strong communication and problem-solving they are working to develop. When our learners face an academic setback—everything from providing an incorrect answer to failing a class—we have the opportunity to lean in and help support a shift in mindset from setback to feedback, from failure to opportunity, and from a negative self-image to growth.

Proactive Strategies

When learners are struggling with an academic setback, their emotions may pose a barrier to the conversation. Ensuring that they are in a space to feel seen, heard, and to listen and engage is important in supporting them to turn the setback into feedback into opportunity. As parents, we can set the stage for these conversations before they happen by being proactive in our communication strategies. Whether as a parent or educator, I dreaded my students' answers to the question, "What did you do in school today?", or, "What did you learn today/yesterday?" When my kids were younger, they would tell me all about the interesting things they learned, where they were stuck, what went wrong, who was nice to them, and what they ate for lunch.

The 9th-grade answers became monosyllabic. "Good," "nothing," and stuff" became stock answers.

I quickly learned that my questions needed to change and evolve with the growing student. I began to make my questions more specific. Questions became a way to engage in a conversation and better understand how their minds were growing, who they were becoming as learners, and what was important to them. Here are a few examples of these questions:

- What was one thing that really annoyed you today?
- What was one kind thing that happened to you or that you observed today?
- What was one kind thing you did today?
- What is one word for how you are feeling about [pick a subject that your student may be struggling with] class?
- What were you proud of today?
- What was one academic risk or chance you took today?
- Where was one place you doubted yourself today?

These are just a few ways to lay the foundation for later conversations that may have more emotion attached. It isn't an interrogation, and you might just pose a single question or time it for a car ride, where kids always seem more willing to talk. In normalizing these conversations, we are validating our students' experiences and the range of emotions that accompany them. Notice that the questions allow space for both celebrating and sharing frustrations.

Educators are using variations of this same technique to build relationships with their students and to help them reflect on their learning and next steps. To gain insight into students' mindsets and to model skills like planning, reflecting, and goal setting, they can ask:

- What are your strengths as a learner?

- When working in a group, what frustrates you and what energizes you?

- How do you best receive feedback?

- How would you score yourself [using this rubric] on the assignment, and what steps might you take to improve that score?

- When do you feel most safe to participate in class?

Parents can also use these questions in strengthening communication and helping their students to recall ideas, skills, and thoughts when faced with an academic setback.

Shifting Mindsets from Setback to Feedback to Opportunity

There are a number of academic moments that will challenge students while they are growing into themselves as young adults, navigating a new school, and also facing increasing rigor and expectations in their coursework. Our 9th graders are struggling for independence, making this an important time for teachers and parents to lean in to offer support and the opportunity to increase ownership, independence, and problem-solving skills. The gradual release of responsibility from parent to child is being mirrored in the classroom, as the educator is releasing increasing responsibility to the student. Teachers will provide scaffolds in the form of outlines, rubrics, and expectations, while supporting the inherent desire of a 9th grader to begin exploring what they are capable of. Not only does this scaffolding strategy increase student engagement, but it also enables them to practice the skills in a safe space that will support their success in high school and beyond.

This increase in student agency throughout 9th grade also manifests in increasing choices for learners to weigh in on their educational experiences. This same approach can be helpful for parents in supporting their child who is experiencing an academic setback. While parents are there to create guardrails, consider the ways that you let your child drive decisions. One strategy is to ask students how they want to be supported. This might sound like a strange question, but as adults we recognize that sometimes the support we are looking for is as simple as someone holding space for us to share concerns. Other times, we ask a trusted friend to help solve a problem, or we want someone to share their experience with an issue. There is not a right answer here; it is about what the student needs to move confidently and successfully forward. As a teacher, if I provided more scaffolding or support than a student needed, I actually risk hindering their learning by helping where it wasn't needed.

When your child is upset and sharing their academic frustration, asking them how they want to be supported is helpful. This might include:

- Just listening
- Asking questions to help the student unpack the experience or feeling
- Brainstorming solutions or next steps (see below)
- Helping to craft an email to the teacher

A teacher might ask some questions when working with a learner after a setback:

- What strategies have you tried where you were successful?
- What supports might help you feel more *organized, productive, clear on expectations,* etc.?
- Would you like *written feedback, a conference, a review session,* or *study strategy ideas?*

Offering options supports learners in building agency and owner-ship of their next steps. This is crucial in building independence and shifting mindsets from "I can't" to "I can't yet." By modeling these strategies, educators and parents lean into the power of yet. This momentary academic setback does not define the learner. Instead, it is a learning opportunity. The setback functions as feedback to improve practice, communication, collaboration, and learning as part of a team, whether parent-student, student-teacher, or parent-student-teacher. Notice how the student is central to all of these conversations. Even as I've emailed one of my own children's teachers, I've noticed a marked change in the effectiveness of the end result when I've included my child in the process, usually by confirming with them that this is the support they want and letting them read or help craft the message.

So far, I've mostly talked about proactive and general strategies to support our students when faced with an academic setback. Next, I'll explore some of the different types of setbacks learners might face and how teachers support these in different ways based on what the learner needs and how they can grow from the experience. Parents can tailor these kinds of support and collaboration at home.

Setbacks in the Classroom

One of the most important initial goals of every teacher is to create an **inclusive, safe classroom culture**. A classroom where students feel ownership and a sense of belonging is foundational to support-ing them to take academic risks. As students enter high school, peer social interactions become dominant influences on identity. However, even with teachers setting up a nurturing classroom culture, some-times interactions happen that are counter to a supportive learning environment. Remember, after all, that we are talking about students who, while they are striving toward being empathetic, kind, inclu-sive young adults, are still learning. Maybe a peer laughed when your child offered an incorrect answer. Perhaps, during a classroom debate, their viewpoint was criticized or attacked in a way that felt personal. Or, during a group collaboration, their ideas were dismissed and they felt shut down by the rest of the group. All of these have the potential to make learners feel no longer safe to take a chance, volunteer their ideas, or participate fully.

So, how can educators and families best support learners faced with a classroom setback of this nature? First, establishing an inclusive, positive classroom culture is not something that is simply a beginning-of-the-term task. Teachers are monitoring the culture of their classroom on a daily and even minute-by-minute basis, because we know that a positive culture is a precondition to meaningful learning. When a teacher observes a classroom setback with a student, they will leverage a variety of techniques tailored to the situation. For example, they might:

- **Validate the idea and participation of the learner.** The teacher reinforces the fact that the student's participation is important and, while their answer might not be there "yet," the volunteered answer might help the class toward a deeper understanding. Learners are valued and mistakes are an expected part of the learning process.

- **Move into the group to model and reinforce expectations.** The teacher may move closer to a group they notice is struggling with maintaining the classroom community expectations. They might join the discussion, modeling productive discourse, where participants agree and disagree. This reminds students that all have an opportunity to have their thoughts heard, corrects those who may not be allowing for other voices, and reestablishes group norms if needed.

- **Remind students about norms and expectations.** While this is most effective as a proactive strategy where students collaborate with the teacher to establish what the classroom should look and feel like, sometimes when harm has been done to the culture, a larger class conversation is facilitated by the teacher. The timing of these conversations depends on the situation and is facilitated in a way that brings attention to the culture, not the individual.

Finally, a teacher might follow up with both the student who caused the harm and, separately, with the student who was impacted. Both are important learning moments for students and reinforce the role all play in creating a safe and engaging learning environment. These private conversations are a cornerstone of strong teacher-student relationships that support the overall classroom environment and allow space for learners to experience setbacks and have an opportunity to grow.

Setbacks Linked to Developing Executive Functioning Skills

Another set of emerging skills that becomes increasingly important as students transition to 9th grade are those that fall under the umbrella of **executive functioning (EF)**. These are a range of skills that help us plan and set goals, initiate tasks, organize, maintain focus, and self-regulate. Teaching students to leverage graphic organizers, agenda books, work plans, and to set goals are all ways to explicitly support the development of these essential skills that many of us take for granted as adults.

While these skills are taught, there is also a gradual release of responsibility to the student, where they demonstrate more control over their choice of tools and support. Where student agendas may have been a universal practice in middle school, students may find themselves having to choose which tool to use (or not) to keep track of their work as they transition into the 9th grade. As a result of increasing autonomy, students can experience academic setbacks that range from missing an assignment because they struggled with task initiation, organizing their work, and creating a plan to complete the work to lacking the organizational skills to know when the work is due.

You may start to notice a pattern to the academic setbacks your student is experiencing. For example, a teacher may notice missing work, incomplete projects, or a struggle to get started on an assignment in class. While the student might feel these are setbacks, as they are always feeling behind, this "setback" is really important "feedback" for the teacher, student, and parent! The teacher will help "diagnose" the root cause of the setbacks with the student in order to recommend ideas to help the learner develop the skills that are lacking. The student can help identify which of these ideas is best suited to their needs. Here are some strategies that a teacher might recommend based on the learner's situation:

Challenge	Recommended learner tools, routines, strategies
Organization	Use agenda book; phone reminders, Google Calendar, or other online calendar; photo of the agenda or homework posted on the board in the classroom
Sustaining attention	Break assignment into chunks; set timer for a period of work and then have a brief reward; create schedule for how time after school is used
Task initiation	Use a graphic organizer; highlight key steps in the directions

What is important here is to uncover the underlying cause of the setback and then support the learner in developing strategies that fit their needs and personality. They will continue to grow and may not need these tools forever, but practicing these strategies at the beginning of high school will help set them up for success as they get older.

The teacher will continue to support your student and keep an eye out for indicators that they are feeling overwhelmed or still falling behind in their work. This might indicate that the strategy needs to be revisited or a deeper collaboration between the teacher and family might be beneficial for supporting and reinforcing consistent strategies both at home and at school.

Setbacks on an Assessment

The last group of setbacks I'll address in this chapter is those a learner might experience on a major assessment like a test, paper, project, lab report, performance, or any other major summative assessment of learning. Putting in effort, trying your best, and taking an academic risk can be scary for a 9th-grade student. After all, what if they do all of this and still don't succeed? Therefore, addressing setbacks becomes critical to help foster a **growth mindset**.

There are two important ideas to unpack here. First, develop a shared understanding with your child of what success looks and feels like. They are likely having this conversation with their teachers about criteria for success, learning outcomes, and how to use a rubric to self-assess ahead of time to set themselves up for success. However, there is another component that is equally important to address: It's easy for students to get caught up in a feeling of competition with others over grades, that As are good and Bs are bad, or even that perfection is the only acceptable outcome. These can be dangerous expectations if they are tied to a student's feelings of self-worth. One approach that many parents and educators take is to emphasize that learning is a journey, where the process of continuous growth, putting forth our best efforts, and leveraging all the resources available to us is what will ultimately help us achieve success.

Your child should work with the teacher to help understand where they were successful and where they may need support or extra practice in order to demonstrate mastery. The teacher may help your child analyze their work, develop a plan to help them improve, and offer a reassessment. It is important for both you and your child to understand school policies so that there are no surprises about the proactive and remedial steps they can take to be afforded these opportunities when needed. Remediation of learning sounds like a negative concept, but at its heart it is about reteaching and providing additional supports and structures to help someone truly demonstrate their knowledge and skills. Great teachers embed much of this proactively into their instructional design. Learners master content at different paces and with different supports. Too often, our children think negatively of themselves if they need additional time or support to master a skill, and so we must remind them that learning is not a race. The teacher will be sharing this same message as they work with your child on a plan for success. Some strategies a teacher may prescribe include:

- Completing corrections on the completed assessment
- Providing an error analysis/rubric review to identify how and where the learner can improve
- Assigning additional practice exercises
- Meeting one-on-one to discuss the assessment together, including specific actionable next steps for improvement

Through the 1:1 conferencing, sometimes teachers and learners discover that the challenge wasn't the content or even the skill being assessed, but the way in which they were being asked to demonstrate their learning. For example, asking learners to demonstrate their understanding and application of a science concept through written expression may limit learners whose writing skills are still developing. This hinders the student's ability to showcase their true understanding of the idea and the teacher's ability to assess it. Through 1:1 conferencing, your child's teacher can better understand what might be inhibiting the student's ability to truly show what they have mastered. The teacher might suggest an alternative assignment, design the assessment with the learner to highlight their understanding, or, as in the case of the written science question, recognize that an oral assessment might be a better tool for understanding where the student is in their learning.

Our children are not one-size-fits-all, and increasingly schools are recognizing this and supporting teachers in leveraging research and best practices to remove barriers to learning and assessment, enabling all students to demonstrate that they can achieve at high levels and that continuous growth should be the celebrated norm, not the exception.

Closing Advice

While the teacher-student-parent partnership looks and feels differently in 9th grade than it did in elementary and middle school, it is no less critical. In 9th grade, students are going to be challenged in new ways that will sometimes feel like setbacks and maybe even failures. Recognizing that internalizing these feelings and negative perceptions of themselves are damaging, we have an incredible opportunity to help students see themselves differently, acknowledge that they might not have it *yet*, and that success can look different than they've thought about it before. Working together, teachers and parents can help students transform their mindset from setback to feedback, from failure to opportunity, and from a negative self-image to a positive one.

Conversation Starters

- Which classrooms do you feel are most inclusive and safe to speak up in and why?

- What is the best way for you to keep track of your assignments?

- How do you know when you should start an assignment?

- How often do you break assignments up into smaller chunks?

- What would be an ideal reward for completing an assignment on time?

- Do you often feel like you need more time or a different way to complete an assessment?

Chapter 8

IS YOUR 9TH GRADER STRUGGLING?

How to support different learning styles and abilities

Barbara Hopkins, PhD
1988 Nebraska State Teacher of the Year

Is your 9th grader struggling in school? If so, whether this is the first time your kid has had struggles or the 18th or the 90th, I am sure you have some anxiety about it, as does your child. It is very difficult to not worry about your child, regardless of their age. And in 9th grade, the stakes feel higher, because grades might impact options for postsecondary education or a job later on.

If you have been in this situation before, remember what worked and what didn't. The first thing to do is to communicate calmly and openly. When a student is struggling, they almost always have anxiety about the situation, regardless of how they appear (or are trying to appear). In my years spent reading my students, many have said they feel like a failure. They do not believe in themselves as learners, don't like school, and have a lot of angst. If any of this sounds familiar, think about what you would need if you were in that situation. Kindness, a calm approach, and respect are key.

In this chapter, I'll explore strategies to use based on your discussions with your 9th grader and their learning style. But first, a review of Maslow's hierarchy of needs might help you to consider if your 9th grader's basic needs are being met.

Maslow's Hierarchy of Needs

Maslow's hierarchy of needs to self-actualization shows five levels:

1. Physical needs, like food and shelter

2. Safety and security

3. Friendship and love

4. Accomplishment and self-esteem

5. Self-actualization through self-awareness and personal growth

Consider each point of Maslow's theory. If your student is eating well (including at school) and has proper shelter, then move on to whether your student feels safe and secure at home and school. Does your student have friendships and feel as though things are okay with friends and family? Is there a sense of accomplishment in some aspect of life (i.e., art, sports, club activities, faith-based groups, music, a particular class)? Accomplishments usually lead to good self-esteem, so reinforce and celebrate the positive. Please do not take away extra-curriculars or classes they love as a way to have more time for subject areas they're not doing well in, or as punishment.

If the basics are there, then you must consider whether the struggle is based on the content, teacher, study habits, or some social situation in or out of school that has not yet been identified. It matters, because your 9th grader has to identify the issue before they can fix it. So think about your approach, as well as some strategies, which I will outline for you.

Identifying the Issue

Picture your 9th grader as a dear little toddler you are tucking into bed at night. Now, envision that toddler becoming a teen, keeping in touch with that same quiet, unconditional love you had for that toddler at bedtime, plus the respect you'd want as a young adult. I remember when someone suggested the "toddler bedtime" visualization to me when my six-foot-two teenager was struggling and I was at my wits' end. It helped me as a parent, and I hope it will help you also.

Step 1: Talk to your child. Using the chart below, try to determine if this is situational, emotional, or truly a problem with learning. Ask:

- Looking at the chart below, what do you think is the major issue(s) you are having?

- Are you experiencing the issue(s) in every class, or is it isolated to a subject area or a particular teacher?

- Is the issue(s) academic or social (meaning an issue with other kids, such as bullying)?

Step 2: Agree on what the major issue is with your 9th grader. This chart lays out some possible issues and how to deal with them.

Issue	Possible Solution	Consider
Overwhelmed with amount of work	Ask how your child organizes class work or studies for tests. Are assignments being tracked in a planner or organizer? Is there enough time to study in a quiet place? Are other activities interfering with study and completing work?	Can you get help with study skills, tutoring, or investigating different learning styles?

(continued)

Issue	Possible Solution	Consider
Content is difficult	Check with the teacher and/or a counselor to see if the student is in the correct course or level. Talk to the educator about having more time to complete tasks, if behind.	Remember long-term goals for postsecondary plans as you adjust course schedules.
Emotional	Ask the counselor about in-school counseling or tutoring. Get advice on how to resolve issues with other students or teachers. Many schools have small group counseling sessions.	Get help for emotional or medical issues through the school or your health care provider. Take care of emotional and mental health like you would a broken arm—you would not ignore it.
Bullying	Get immediate assistance from a teacher, counselor, and administrator as needed to resolve the issue. Call or email as advised by the school, but respond quickly.	Schools typically have very strict rules about bullying, because it can impair a student's learning.

(continued)

Issue	Possible Solution	Consider
Concerns about the teacher	Begin with the teacher. If that does not resolve the issue or you need a mediator (or assistance), include a school administrator. Will moving to a different class or dropping the class solve the problem?	There are times to make changes in your environment and times to make changes within institutional environments.

Learning Styles

Over the years, researchers have identified different learning styles, as well as various assessments of these learning styles, depending on what a student is learning. Below is a chart of different learning styles so you can help your 9th grader think about how they best learn, which may impact how they approach their classes, study, take notes, and interact with others to aid in their learning.

Learning Style	Characteristics	Study Strategies
Visual	Using pictures, images, and spatial understanding	Use a white board or make notes by turning words or ideas into images or pictures to learn and remember. Draw out concepts into a storyboard (like cartoon squares that tell a story).

(continued)

Learning Style	Characteristics	Study Strategies
Aural	Auditory-musical: using sound and music	After taking notes, turn the ideas into music or a poem or relate it to a story to aid in recall of key details. Turn the lesson into a song or dance so that when you visualize the dance or remember the song, you recall the information.
Verbal	Linguistic: using words	Verbalize the lesson in your own words. Maybe record it into a device (i.e., phone) to help memorize.
Physical	Kinesthetic: using the body, hands, and sense of touch	Make a sculpture or draw in sand to help remember key concepts. Come up with physical gestures that relate to the class content (i.e., toddlers often have hand motions to go with songs, which is using the body to aid in learning).

(continued)

Learning Style	Characteristics	Study Strategies
Logical	Mathematical: using logic and reasoning	Use recognition of patterns and connections of concepts, as well as numbers. Turn key concepts into mathematical equations (i.e., Romeo + Juliet = disaster).
Social	Interpersonal: working in groups	Organize a study group or find a study partner to bounce ideas off each other.
Solitary	Intrapersonal: working alone	Arrange a quiet space (if desired) to study alone, and take time to concentrate on the class content, attaching it to feelings, previous experiences, and thoughts.

Closing Advice

Consider the 9th grader's hierarchy of needs to assess anything that could be interfering with learning and causing struggles. Above all, love your 9th grader as you always have and be patient, as the start of high school is a new path to navigate. Consider their learning style and ways to adapt or adjust to address whatever the struggle might be. Access the help that is available from the school, educators, counselors, and administration. Everyone wants your 9th grader to succeed.

Conversation Starters

- In the classes you enjoy, what makes them enjoyable?

- What do you think your greatest strengths are? What are you really good at? How can you apply those skills to what you are struggling with?

- What are you most proud of about yourself? (You can follow up with, "I am proud of you because you are _____.")

- How do you like to study? By yourself or with others? Can you name a few kids in each of your classes that you could study with?

- Is high school easier, harder, or about the same as middle school? What makes it that way?

- When you are a senior in high school, what do you hope is different? What do you hope is the same?

Chapter 9

CHALLENGING STUDENT-TEACHER RELATIONSHIPS

Questions, scenarios, advice, and scripts

Jada Reeves
2019 West Virginia State Teacher of the Year

Am I really old enough to have a kid in high school? How did these years go by so fast? Wasn't my child just crawling and in diapers? These are questions you probably ask yourself during this critical transition time. You are watching your teen move from an awkward middle school kid into the independence that high school creates. If these questions are not enough to make you crazy, this vital year, when your child enters 9th grade, may make you teeter on the edge of an emotional breakdown because...YOUR. BABY. IS. ENTERING. HIGH. SCHOOL! YIKES.

This chapter will provide support to the questions you may have and the challenges your teenager may face as a freshman in high school.

The key to helping your 9th grader have a successful first year of high school, and with their life's pertinent changes (and your own turmoil of changes), is patience, grace, and a little more patience.

Helping Your Teen Become Independent at School

Whether or not we are ready, our babies are entering high school. This critical transition period is one of the most stressful situations your child will experience. Your teen's emotions will be one major roller-coaster ride on some days! Academic classes in high school are more difficult with more homework, and teens are learning how to balance this new chapter in their lives. On top of a new school with new teachers comes new friends and new extracurricular activities. One role we have as parents is to help them become independent and deal with issues independently as they arise. It is difficult to sit back and not intervene, but teenagers must learn to manage challenging situations in high school with and without parental support.

Listen

Those moods, though, ugh…. Your teen has much to say, even if their mood and face show otherwise. The first step in becoming supportive and expecting your teen to alleviate challenging student-teacher relationships is to listen. Provide a safe place for your teen to talk, open up, and tell you what is going on. You need to get the full picture of what is happening in class so you can provide insightful advice on the daunting learning environment of 9th grade.

I know it is hard to listen and not intervene; I have teenagers myself. However, kids entering 9th grade are still learning to develop their morals and ethical compasses. No longer are they the self-centered middle schoolers you came to tolerate. These new creatures you currently house are aware of their surroundings, making sense of the world and how relationships work. One of the relationships they are now cognizant of is how their personal life affects school and the challenges they may experience with educators.

Patience and Questions

"If you think that being a great parent requires limitless patience, you are wrong. You need more than that."—Unknown

Teenagers will test your patience more times than you care to count. However, showing your teens grace and patience requires... well... it requires patience. After you have provided ample time in listening to your teen voice their concerns, it is time to ask questions.

1. When did this issue start?

2. Have you spoken to the teacher?

3. What did the teacher say?

4. Have you tried to do what the teacher told you?

5. What else should you do?

Ensuring the questions you ask your teen are open-ended allows your teen to process the situation and take ownership of the dilemma.

Challenging student and teacher relationships can be exhausting. However, holding your teen accountable by helping them reflect and use open-ended questioning will aid in developing a responsible student who is equipped with problem-solving skills for the real world.

Respect

Reflect on when you were a teenager. What was the most important thought you had? Most likely, it was about your friends. Friends are your teen's entire world right now. They will most likely prefer friends over family if they had to choose. When teenagers hang out with their friends, they talk and they listen. They automatically seem to listen and support each other with situations because they can relate. That is part of the respect teens need to feel with adults, too. Teenagers crave peer acceptance, but this acceptance relates to the respect they feel when they interact with each other.

Just like adults need to feel accepted and respected, teenagers are now emerging into young adults. They also need to feel respected and that their parents and teachers value their emerging individuality. Teenagers desire power over their lives and want to feel in control of what may happen at school. It is your job to step in and show your teen how to deal with difficult relationships that may hinder their identity, which is slowly evolving.

Space, Space, and More Space

What is space? The space you provide your teen allows them to grapple with ideas to alleviate their problem because they are now self-aware and capable of reflecting on situations and how to handle them based on prior experiences. This step requires your consistent patience. Your teen may not address the teacher the very next day. Sometimes teenagers must process the information and acquire the courage to confront the teacher if they are having issues. As the parent, you may need to provide motivation, reassurance, and a little prodding until the teenager tries to rectify their challenge. Allowing that much-needed space gives your teen the opportunity to problem-solve on their own because they now encompass more complex thinking skills.

Follow Up

After allowing your teen to problem-solve, it is vital to provide a follow-up discussion with them on the progress or attempts they made with the troublesome relationship. Leaving them to take care of it and not checking back in may cause the teen to feel isolated. Conducting a subsequent conversation about how the discussion with the teacher went demonstrates to your teen that you care about them, along with giving your teen an accountability measure to follow through with the task.

Example Scenarios

Scenario One: Assignment Homework—Student to Teacher

Many times, students are scared to ask a teacher why they received a grade they did. Ensuring your teen phrases the question so it is not negatively intended is key. Practice using the example below with your teen when they miss a question and feel the answer they provided is valid.

"Could you please help me see why this answer is incorrect? I thought it was right because...."

Scenario Two: Student Emotions

Teenage brains are scrambled. No, really, they are! Kids in 9th grade really struggle to regulate their brains to decipher which emotion is which. Teens tend to use accusatory words (i.e., "My teacher is terrible."), deflection strategies (i.e., "If my teacher would just..."), or feel attacked (i.e., "I didn't do anything wrong!"), because they just do not know how to get the correct feelings into words. Teenagers are naturally self-centered, so they honestly do not consider how the teacher with whom they have disengaged feels.

Try these questions to support your teen in recognizing the correct emotion they are experiencing so that you assist correctly.

- "You seem angry. What happened that made you so mad?"
- "I see that you are crying. I know being a teenager is tough. Tell me what happened during the school day that made you so sad."

- "Tell me what upset you at school so we can determine your feelings."

- "Give me an example of something your teacher does that frustrates you."

- "Now that we know you are feeling _____, have you told your teacher how you feel?"

- "How should you and I respond to this feeling?"

- "Are you tired or stressed? Sometimes lying down helps you feel rejuvenated, so you are not so anxious."

- "Okay, you want to be left alone right now. Let me know when you are ready to talk."

Scenario Three: Vibe Jibe

Your teenager may come to you and express their frustrations about a certain teacher because they do not "vibe." Teenagers can feel the energy, and student and teacher personalities clash sometimes. Rehearse the following phrases with your 9th grader so they can address the teacher to disseminate those "negative feels."

- "Ms. Williams, can I talk to you privately sometime?"

- "Ms. Williams, I want to do well in your class but need to do something different to succeed. Please help me and tell me if there is anything I can do to be a better student in your class."

There may be times when you will need to encourage your teen to talk to the guidance counselor at their school about this situation. Counselors are trained to help your teen solve problems on their own. Parents are always welcome to email or call the school to speak to the counselor and make them aware of the situation. As a last resort, use the administrator as a point of contact. Waiting until you, your teen, the teacher, and the counselor have exhausted all options demonstrates that everyone has tried to remedy the situation with strategies before involving the principal.

Scenario Four: Grading Timely

With the development of internet-based grading systems, parents immediately have access to their teen's grades. There are pros and cons to this. Teachers may create an assignment for the students to complete, and the due date is later, but the assignment shows the points missing from their final grade. This frequent scenario causes unrest and anxiety for both the parent and the student. Try practicing the following sentence prompts with your teen so they can figure out how their teacher inputs grades and assignments.

- "I turned in my assignment on_____, but the grade book is showing my work still needs to be graded. Did you see my submission?"
- "My parent(s) saw I had a zero on an assignment I turned in. When will it be graded so that my final grade reflects my submitted work?"

If this tactic does not work with your teen addressing the teacher themselves, then it is okay to email the teacher yourself to ask.

Hi, Ms. Williams, I was curious about the assignment that Jane turned in on _____. The low grade worried us, and I wanted to see when the assignment would be graded to reflect her final grade. Jane knows we value education and will have consequences at home if she does not complete her work. I was following up on my conversation with her to ensure we were on the same page and to see if there was something I could do to help her, if needed. I appreciate all the hard work teaching teens all day!

Examples That Need Direct Parent Intervention

Although our role as parents is to prepare our teens for the real world and encourage them to try and resolve any issues that may arise with their teacher on their own, there are times when direct parent intervention is necessary. Knowing their parents are always there for them and can step in if needed provides security for teens. Your first step is contacting the specific teacher. Speaking to the teacher first allows them to know the situation and gives you a chance to address any needs with where the problem lies. Before contacting the teacher directly, keep the following ideas in mind to help you remain positive with the educator who has your teen every day, yet is supportive in meeting your teen's needs.

- Respect the teacher's authority and time.
- Request a meeting in person via email. Refrain from negative reactions in your message.
- Avoid name-calling.
- Speak kindly of the teacher in the teen's presence.

If you are still determining what warrants direct parent intervention, remember the following issues. These situations require the parent to step in immediately.

1. If a student has been threatened or harmed in any way

2. Your teen is falling behind, or their grades have declined

3. If your teen's attempts at communicating with the teacher are futile and have not worked

4. Your teen is being disrespected, embarrassed, or belittled in class

If the endeavors do not produce positive results in communicating with the teacher, it is essential to move to the next step—contacting the administrator. Using the principal as the next step for direct parent intervention provides time for the teacher to respond. It renders respect for the teacher's authority in adhering to their promises. Requesting to meet with the principal when they are available shows that you are concerned about an issue with your teen but also respectful of the administrator's time. Most days, the main administrator has meetings set up previously or may be out of the building. Asking for a meeting time about the specific issue shows flexibility and readies you and the school to be prepared to discuss your concerns in a timely manner.

When it is time for your meeting with the administrator, be prepared. Take your notes, correspondences with the teacher, and any concerns you have to stay focused in the meeting. Ensure that you start the meeting by telling everyone involved that you are thankful for the encounter so you all can work together to ensure your teen is successful in school.

Parent-Student Scripts for Speaking with Teachers

Example Script 1: Email from Parent to Teacher

Hi Ms. Williams,

I am Jane's mother. She is a student in your 7th-period math class. I have a few items that I would like to discuss with you in person or over the phone. Is there a time you can speak with me this week? My cell is 111-222-3333. Please feel free to call or text me at that number or reply to this email.

I appreciate your time and attention!

Sincerely,

Joy Jones

Example Script 2: Phone Call Message from Parent to Teacher

Hello,

My name is Joy Jones, and I was calling to speak with Ms. Williams. She is my daughter's 9th-grade math teacher in 7th period. Could you give her my cell and have her call me when she is available, please? I had a concern over a grade Jane received on a recent assignment. My cell is 111-222-3333.

Thanks so much!

Example Script 3: Email from Student to Teacher

Ms. Williams,

I need help with the assignment on using a winter scene and writing an excerpt using imagery and personification. It has not snowed here recently, and the assignment said the picture used could not be clip art or something from the internet.

Jane

Example Script 4: In-person Conversation between Student and Teacher

Ms. Williams, it is hard for me to sit still in class at my desk because we have a double block. My legs are going numb, and it makes me lose focus. Can I sit in the back of the room so I can stand as long as I am still doing my work? I promise I will not be a distraction.

Closing Advice

What a thrilling ride parenting a teenager can be! If no one has told you lately, you are doing a good job! Sometimes we cannot see the light at the end of the tunnel because we hit a pothole in the parenting journey. At times, we must pick ourselves and our teens up, dust everyone off, keep going, and try again. This example you set for your teen exhibits resilience.

You are demonstrating excellent parenting seeking assistance in developing and molding your 9th grader by digesting this book. I wish you luck traveling on the journey of parenting a teenager and navigating them through challenging student-teacher relationships.

Chapter 10
PARENT-EDUCATOR COMMUNICATION

How can you work with school personnel to support student achievement?

Jennifer Skomial
2019 New Jersey State Teacher of the Year

Family and school partnerships ensure success for all learners. In the elementary grades, parent involvement opportunities are in abundance. Parent volunteers are often asked to read to their children's classes, organize themed parties, and, of course, attend events such as concerts and field days. Back-to-school nights and conferences provide opportunities for partnering with school staff. However, as students move from elementary to middle school, opportunities for parent involvement lessen. Parents often see the opportunities to get involved at the high school level as nonexistent. Many families struggle to know just when to provide support and when to encourage independence during freshman year of high school.

This transition creates an unknown territory for parents and guardians to navigate. When freshman year begins, students are often seeking opportunities to show that they are capable of making decisions for themselves and handling their own schoolwork, yet they are conditioned to the comforts they were provided in middle school from both teachers and their parents. It becomes a delicate balance of letting a teenager explore this new world of high school while ensuring they make good choices and feel supported when it is most needed.

Despite the slow release of responsibility that occurs during freshman year of high school, family and school partnerships are still critical to a child's achievement in school. Let's take a look at some ways families can connect with key staff members to support their student's achievement.

Classroom Teachers

As a freshman, your child will have between six and 12 different teachers. Because each classroom teacher will likely have different expectations, it is important for your child to know and understand how each one conducts their classroom. This will soon become second nature to your child, as they will be in that person's classroom several times a week. However, each educator's procedures will be foreign to you, as a parent. Back to School Night or another beginning of the year event is an ideal time to receive information about the courses your child is taking and to get a snapshot of what it will be like for your child to be in each class. While this will not be the time for individual discussions and feedback about your child, you can introduce yourself, gather handouts, and get a sense of what your child will be learning throughout the year.

Part of supporting your child during this transitional year is knowing when to have them advocate for themselves and when it's appropriate for you to step in. Whenever there is a discrepancy over a grade, question about an assignment, or personal update to share, it is always best for your child to talk with the teacher in person. A person's tone is often lost via email, so the best way to communicate will be face-to-face. If it is difficult to speak privately with the teacher, or the student needs a quick answer while home for a period of time, the student should send a businesslike email. In most cases, it is best for the student to take this step, not the parent. The email should mention the concern and ask for a time to meet to discuss. The student should not expect to resolve an important issue via email. If, however, the student does not receive an adequate response when they meet in person, or there is a more significant concern to share with the teacher, such as a death in the family or the need for the child to be out sick for an extended period of time, it would be appropriate for the parent to send an email.

Example Email from Student:

Dear Mr. Campbell,

I had hoped to talk with you today about my most recent quiz grade. Unfortunately, I had to rush off to catch my bus. Could we talk tomorrow during my lunch at 11:15?

Thanks for your time,

Matthew

Example Email from Parent:

Dear Mr. Campbell,

I hope this email finds you well. Jasmine has been struggling lately after the loss of her grandmother. I wanted to inform you in case you notice any impact on her academics. Her guidance counselor is also aware.

Thank you for your help,

Ms. Thomas

Classroom Volunteers/Guest Speakers

At the high school level, one way to stay involved in your child's education is to become a guest speaker. Teachers are often looking for professionals to speak with students, and you might be able to share a skill or the story of your career path with a group of students. Other opportunities to volunteer might include chaperoning an event, coordinating fundraising, or assisting with a large-scale project. During Back to School Night, tell your child's teacher(s) that you'd like to get involved as a guest speaker. You can follow up with an email to remind the teacher and to provide contact information.

Guidance Counselor

In most high schools, students are assigned to one guidance counselor for all four years. Your child's guidance counselor will be an invaluable resource for the selection of classes, college planning, and social-emotional needs. If your child is struggling greatly with a particular course or realizes an elective is not the right fit, they should meet with their counselor. You can always follow up with an email to ensure the counselor knows you are supportive of any changes.

Consider reaching out to your child's guidance counselor if a life-altering event occurs, because they may be able to put you in touch with grief counselors, therapists, and tutors. You can also ask a guidance counselor to share news and updates with your child's teachers. This alleviates the need for you to field replies from teachers and allows you to focus on your family's needs. The guidance counselor can be the main point of contact in these more serious situations.

For matters that are less serious in nature, have your child communicate with their counselor just as they would their teachers. This is a great opportunity to give guidance yet also teach independence.

Don't write an email for your child. Instead, sit together to type it out or have your child show it to you for revisions before hitting send. Or provide a sentence starter and have your child finish it. For example, "I would like to talk with you after lunch about an issue with...." If you'd like to stay in the loop, have your child copy you on the email. Almost any concern you or your child has should be shared with your child's counselor. This individual should work to coordinate efforts behind the scenes to provide additional support.

Child Study Team

In some cases, students need an additional layer of support in order to be successful in school. This is especially true for students who require accommodations and/or modifications in the classroom. This level of support should be communicated between a student's family and case manager. At the beginning of the school year, or even sooner, a parent should advocate for their child's needs via email to their point of contact on the child study team. This team consists of some or all of the following professionals: school psychologists, school social workers, learning disabilities teachers/consultants, and speech-language specialists. These professionals will be useful to your child during school hours and can help connect you with resources outside of school, such as occupational therapists, psychological services, and even transitional services to prepare students for job-related experiences. As changes occur throughout the year, send updates via email. While a phone call is often more personal and can help individuals discuss matters more deeply, it is always important to follow up in writing.

Example Email from Parent:

Dear Mrs. Quincy,

I appreciate your time today to discuss Hunter's upcoming IEP meeting. I'm glad that we'll be able to address some of his needs in more detail at that meeting. Thank you for communicating his current struggles with his teachers. We will see you in two weeks.

Sincerely,

Jessica Zoback

School Nurse

The school nurse can be an essential partner in your child's overall health and wellness. Communicating with the school nurse can help ensure that staff members understand any conditions your child may have, as well as any health concerns that occur along the way, such as an injury. Not only will the nurse ensure all concerns and protocols are shared with educators when possible, but she will also check in with your child periodically to see how they are doing. The nurse can be another staff member for your child to seek out when extra support is needed.

Coaches/Athletic Director/Club Advisors

If your child is involved in extracurricular activities such as sports or Model Congress, you should try to get to know your child's coaches and advisors. Coaches will be instrumental during your child's time on a team, and they will help your child balance sports and academics. After-school activities offered by the school, such as Key Club, National Honor Society, and photography club, will be advised by one or two staff members. Opening the lines of communication with a coach or club advisor can be useful if your child is starting to struggle to keep up with their grades and the demands of these activities.

In the long term, these adults might help when it comes to the college process. A coach can help guide an athlete in deciding which college will provide the best possible experience in terms of playing a particular sport. Club advisors also might help steer a kid toward summer opportunities and colleges. Both advisors and coaches could write letters of recommendation, if they know a student well. Discussing future goals will benefit your child in many ways.

Talking with a coach and/or athletic director will help you find ways to get more involved. One way would be to volunteer with the booster club—which fundraises for the sports teams—or other organized groups. Clubs also host special events and might need parent involvement.

Principals/Vice Principals

Principals and vice principals have a much higher view of all that goes on within a school. Partnering with administration could help put you in touch with other staff members who will be able to support your child during 9th grade. Additionally, there is always a need for parent volunteers to serve on advisory groups, sponsor events, share an area of expertise, or put their skills to use. Reaching out to an administrator and sharing your desire to get involved will help them know who to reach out to when a parent perspective is needed.

Closing Advice

While it can seem intimidating to get to know a whole new group of teachers, counselors, coaches, and administrators, know that they want what's best for your child. And while building independence is the first goal of 9th grade, you can still be in close contact with the adults who spend a considerable amount of time with your child. The main goal is to support your child's academic and high school career. You can use this list of dos and don'ts to guide you:

DOs

- Speak respectfully about school and staff members, because children learn what they see.

- Model how to have a conversation with adults. If your child is struggling to have a conversation with their guidance counselor, for example, have them practice with you, because role-playing is a great way to get more comfortable.

- Check the grading portal with your child every couple of days and then move to once a week. Eventually, have your child do the checking to ensure all assignments are up to date. It's easier to catch an issue with a grade if it's done early and not at the end of a marking period.

- Provide enough time for a response before emailing a teacher again or going to an administrator.

- Follow the chain of command when there is an issue (student to teacher, parent to teacher, parent to administrator).

- Ensure your child is setting time aside, without distractions, to study and complete homework. They need this structure from an adult.

DON'Ts

- Make assumptions or accusations about teachers or other staff members before hearing both sides of the story

- Reach out immediately on your child's behalf, because this is a great time to help your child become independent

- Call or text your child when they're in class. Whether you need to ask about a grade or how your child will get home after school, it's crucial to reinforce that your child stays focused in class. Reach out during lunch.

Chapter 11
ONLINE DAZE

The science behind technology and your 9th grader

Jim Shaner
STEM/Science Teacher, Ohio

Eric, our fictional 9th grade student, begins his day by checking his Snapchat stories to see if anyone has posted anything important yet that morning. He doubts that he has missed much, because he was up late playing Call of Duty on Xbox Live with his crew. Eric's TikTok FYP (For You Page) is pulled up while he goes to the bathroom. He scrolls through and likes a couple of videos as he continues getting ready for school. AirPods in, YouTube playlist in the background, Eric waits for the bus to school.

It has been a little less than two hours since he woke up, and he has been engaged with social media and apps the entire time. Throughout the day, our fictional student will spend hours on social media; hours in front of an interactive screen. The 9th grader has never known a world without modern technology. Google has been around since

1996. YouTube made its debut in 2005. The iPhone came out in June 2007. (Facebook started in 2006, though few teens would be caught dead using that service today.) Eric and his peers have been connected to one another since they got their first cell phones. They are always carrying a small computer, never more than a few clicks away from any information or entertainment they could ever desire.

Surrounded by tech from birth, these technophiles cannot imagine a world without the buzz of notifications, without connection to the web. Their brains have been conditioned from an early age to expect the constant stimulation of unexpected events provided by their electronic devices; the real world seems bland by comparison. Try to take the phone away from a 9th grader and you will get a visceral response, because experiencing life without this constant interaction is apparently terrifying. Fear will soon turn to anger as the addict loses their source of dopamine. No longer surrounded by notifications, updates, and new Snapchats, your child's sense of fairness, or, more precisely, the lack of fairness in this cruel, cruel world, will cause them to lash out.

Tech Work-Arounds

The more clever teens may find work-arounds to maintain communication with their friends, whether through sideloading apps onto their phone, using the chat feature on their Xbox, or purchasing a new charging cord to replace the cord that you so cleverly took away. Another tool available to bypass restrictions would be the use of a virtual private network (VPN) to mask their activity. VPNs create an encrypted tunnel that allows the user to bypass content blocks, website restrictions, and parental controls. Even the proposed federal bans on social media could be bypassed by using a VPN and changing the country that the device thinks it is located in.

Try to think of these work-arounds as your child exercising critical thinking and problem-solving skills. Recall all of the clever work-arounds that you created to get around punishments as a teen. If you find yourself having to use the loss of phone privileges or web access as a punishment for a 9th-grade student, keep this paradigm in mind. Keep a sense of humor and remember that the world has changed significantly since you were wriggling your way out of punishments from the adults in your life. Ensure you set a limit for how long the tech will be out of reach. Allow for ways to earn back access. Consider allowing limited access that increases incrementally as behavior improves. Your teen has never known a world without being connected, so it will be almost as if they've lost their sense of sight or hearing. They will need to be trained on how to do homework and find information in the ancient ways of the late 1900s.

The "late 1900s" is an unfathomable, backward era where one was unreachable for hours at a time and where answers required effort to find. The modern student has moved beyond using Google to search for information. Web searches can be used to find the answers to entire homework assignments; apps like Photomath can be used to solve math problems, and ChatGPT can be used to write papers. The connected world can be leveraged to find quick answers so that focus can be turned to more enjoyable pursuits.

The teenage brain is results-driven. Taking shortcuts to get things done allows students to move on to what they really want to do. The freshman might ask, "Why should I write this paper when I can copy and paste what somebody else has written?", or, "Why should I waste my time working on this math proof when it's already done for me?" This same student will wonder why they do poorly on tests when they "completed" all the homework. The still-developing teenage brain may equate this failure with a lack of ability and give up on the process of education.

Sources and Critical Thinking

Your 9th grader will need to be taught how to properly evaluate sources of information. Any primate can be taught to make a convincing-looking website, but that does not mean that the information presented is reliable. Look at who publishes the site: Does the individual or organization have an ulterior motive for publishing it? Use the Wayback Machine found at archive.org to look at what the website looked like in previous iterations. Ask yourself if the author is credible. Is there a website or email available that the reader can use to learn more information or contact the author? Spelling and grammar errors can be red flags regarding trustworthiness of information. Check to see if the information can be verified by other legitimate sources. Additional questions to consider: How well-maintained is the site? Do the links still work? Does the page show when it was last updated?

Young adults will continue developing the ability to think critically throughout their high school years. Thinking will move from concrete operations to more logical thought processes. Encourage your student to participate in **metacognition**, which is thinking about thinking. Have them explain *how* they solved a problem, what strategies were used, and how they might fine-tune these in the future.

Teens need a safe environment where they can take chances. Encourage your child to try different activities and to be involved in new extracurricular activities. Cognitive scientists from MIT have discovered that conversations can change the structure of a growing brain. Collaborate with your child to solve a problem. Model a spirit of inquiry about the world around you.

Short-Term vs. Long-Term Thinking

The prefrontal cortex is still developing in freshmen. Most decisions are made in the emotional center of the brain, the amygdala. Thinking long-term is a foreign concept to the 9th-grade student.

Students need instruction on how to think critically and feedback on how to improve thought processes.

The student who uses websites or apps to complete homework without understanding it is falling victim to shortsighted thinking. Photomath and apps like it can be used to model how to construct mathematical proofs. Real learning occurs when the student can apply that knowledge to construct proofs of their own.

A change in perspective can help writing aids and AI become instruments for better writing instead of ways to cheat. ChatGPT can be used to write papers but could be better used to model what good writing looks like. Copying and pasting information from a web page that I don't understand only makes me look stupid when the teacher asks me about a reference that I obviously didn't write. Summarizing and rewording that information allows me to incorporate that knowledge and grow as a learner.

The Emotional Impact of Social Media

The amygdala as the problem-solving center of the developing brain also explains why social media has such a hold over 9th-grade students (and the rest of us!). The emotional response center of the brain predictably reacts emotionally to situations. Students need to be taught how to apply logic and react rationally to situations. They need to learn better ways to deal with people who upset them, rather than putting them on blast on TikTok or uploading unflattering pictures of them to Instagram. Pictures shared, social media rants, or statements made on Wikis could affect the growing teen into adulthood; the internet is forever. A former student of mine lost a full-ride athletic scholarship to college due to some racist things that he said on Twitter. AI facial recognition is getting better at matching up people with images and videos found online, even when the person is not tagged. Ninth-grade students seldom consider that anything placed on the internet could be viewed by future employers, work colleagues, or their curious future children. It's also easy to be an internet troll behind a keyboard and to forget that if they are targeting someone, they are a real person who can be hurt. Too many have been scarred, or worse, from online abuse.

I'm glad that I did not have to deal with the dangers of social media when I was growing up. Today, students are bombarded with images of physical perfection. Knowing that filters exist and that everyone uses filters does not change the perception that what one sees in the mirror is not good enough compared to those images found on social media. A student's entire feeling of self-worth could be related to how many likes a post gets and how many reactions their newest Snapchat garners.

Navigating Social Media

Parenting a 9th grader includes helping them to navigate the minefield of social media perfection and cyberbullying. Do your best to learn how social media sites like TikTok, Instagram, and Snapchat work. Have your teen show you their profiles. Try to set limits on social media usage; you may want to limit where social media can be used or set time limits for access to those sites. Your teen can use this attention as social cover when they really don't feel like replying to a late-night message from a friend. Every teen will relate when your kid explains that it's their parents' fault. Talk to your 9th grader honestly about online matters and build trust with them so that they will tell you times when they are uncomfortable with something that happens online. Do not blame your teen or dismiss the incident. Save copies of the interactions and bring your concerns to the school or, in extreme cases, to law enforcement.

Navigating Learning Management Systems

Guiding a 9th grader will also involve helping them to navigate the myriad of communication tools used by school districts. As with social media, become familiar with the different tools available. Ask your teen questions and make sure you understand where different information is available and how to use the tools available. Learning management systems (LMS) allow teachers to post classwork and resources and for students to submit completed coursework. Popular options include Google Classroom, Blackboard, and Canvas.

Parent portals allow a school to post important information and forms, upload documents, and allow parents to check on student progress. Schools may use different tools to communicate with parents: Higher grades may use Remind 101, Flipgrid, or Google Classroom, while younger grades may use ClassDojo or Bloomz. Parents with more than one student within the same school district may have to use multiple platforms to keep track of communications from different grade levels, though many districts are attempting to streamline communications.

Closing Advice

The world that your 9th grader experiences is not the same one that you experienced as a freshman. They have never known a world without social media, interactive screens, and constant immersion in technology. Today's teens will spend several hours per day on social media; they may place their entire sense of self-worth on the whims of online likes or shares. Be present, engaged, and proactive in teaching your teen to think critically. They need to be loved and supported in order to grow to their fullest potential in today's tech-drenched world.

Questions for Reflection

- How can you help your teen learn to think critically? How can you model critical evaluation of online information sources?

- What limits should be placed on technology/social media use? Would it be appropriate to collaborate with your teen to create guidelines?

- How do you balance the need for your 9th grader to be able to confide in you with their desire for increasing independence?

- How can the online tools offered by the school district be used to hold your teen accountable and to allow them to self-regulate and pursue their goals?

Conversation Starters

- How do you decide if an online information source is giving you good, unbiased information?

- Is it wrong to copy and paste information found on the web into reports? Is it okay to use sites and apps to find the answers to homework questions? How can you use these resources to help you understand the questions better (rather than just getting things done)?

- What is something that someone said to you, or that you've seen, online that made you uncomfortable?

- How do you know that you are doing well in class? Where do you look?

Chapter 12
OUT OF SCHOOL

What should you do if your child must be absent?

Heidi Edwards
Physical Science and AP Biology Teacher, Ohio

The dreaded "I don't feel good" first thing in the morning sets the stage for a chaotic beginning to the day. You are quickly trying to evaluate the situation. Are they sick enough to stay home? Do you send them to school and hope for the best? While how to handle an illness is a family decision, an absence from high school can become a chance for students to learn to advocate for themselves.

Get to Know the Teachers and High School Expectations

Building relationships with the teachers is a key component for high school success. Most schools will hold an open house or preview night prior to or at the beginning of the school year, so you can meet your student's teachers. Aside from putting names with faces, this is an opportunity to learn about classroom structure and procedures. Learning about the amount of homework to expect, what class materials are needed, and the course design is how you begin to understand how to best support your student, both while they are at school or when they are absent.

As a product of the COVID-19 pandemic, digital technology has been incorporated into many classrooms, so ask how the teacher uses these instructional tools and how to access them remotely. Ask if the teacher provides a weekly agenda with which the student can cross-check homework on a nightly basis and turn to in the event of an absence. The answers to these questions will not only give you instructional insight, but will also allow you to more effectively understand communications between the teacher and your student.

This is also a great time to encourage students to introduce themselves and get to know their teachers. Most teachers at the secondary level will be seeing well over 100 students in a day, so establishing the name-face connection is very helpful. Students need to understand that teachers are there to assist them in their journey, but at this stage in their education, they need to become advocates for themselves. If a student is unclear on directions, has a question, isn't understanding content, or is struggling after an absence, it is up to the student to ask. This is an area where many struggle. Advocacy is an important life skill and one that you can help nurture.

High school is a big jump from middle school or junior high and will be an adjustment for your student. The transition to a higher level of autonomy is an opportunity for growth but also a hurdle for some students. The move to more course offerings and an environment where students are moving between classrooms lays the groundwork for potential academic hurdles if absences occur. Each teacher will have their own classroom structure, expectations, and processes for handling absences. Even if you have had previous kids go through the school, staffing changes from year to year and classroom expectations can also change from one course to another taught by the same teacher. Invest time on communication with your student's teachers.

Be in Touch and Schedule Make-Up Sessions

How to handle an absence is a key lifelong skill that you can model for your student. Schools will have a reporting system for absences, so acquaint yourself with that phone number. While you call in to report the absence, ask your student to take responsibility for their schoolwork while they are out. When they are feeling well enough to hop on their school laptop, have the student email their teachers and copy you. This reinforces the fact that your student is responsible for what happens in the classroom when they are out, which is similar to what will be expected once they enter the workforce. Many teachers will appreciate the communication and may be able to provide an update to the lesson for the day or direct students to resources and materials that they can use to catch up upon their return to the classroom.

Probably the most common assumption of students is that the world stops when they are not at school. They assume that they are not responsible for content or classwork for the missed day, and nothing is further from the truth. In science classes, this can be difficult, especially if the student was absent for a lab. Not all labs can be made up; sometimes the student must just obtain data to complete the lab analysis, but it is on the student to ask for and secure that data. In math, students may be working with manipulatives that help explain the class content, and the student may need to set up a time with the teacher to come in and work through those materials. Every classroom is different, and it is the student's responsibility to see how and what needs to be made up.

Students need to understand that a day or more out of school may require make-up time during lunch, before/after school, or during a study hall period. This is not a punishment, but time that might be needed to catch up on missed lessons. Contacting teachers to set up these make-up sessions is important. I have had students choose not to make up work, and then write on a unit evaluation that they were not at school for the content, as if they will receive a free pass. You may be physically excused from school for the day, but you are not academically excused from the content that you missed. Especially in courses such as math and science, where content builds from one day to the next, a day's absence with no make-up effort can turn into a substantial missed learning opportunity that is hard to recover from. Ninth-grade students often learn this lesson the hard way. While some teachers will reach out, the sheer number of students they are working with, and the number of absent students they manage, really shifts accountability to the student.

Students with Special Services

What if your student has an Individualized Education Program (IEP) or is using a 504 plan to receive services through special education or the guidance department? The staff monitoring these services are great resources to help catch up your student, re-explain missed content, and help prioritize work when they have been absent. These teachers and support staff provide another key line of communication into the regular education classroom. Even if your student is being served by an IEP/504, I would highly encourage you to help them develop these self-advocacy skills.

Types of Absences

There are a number of types of absences: appointments, chronic illness, school-excused absences such as field trips, and sick days.

Try to avoid scheduling appointments during core classes such as math, social studies, science, or English, if possible. Knowing your student's schedule is useful, because if you can schedule appointments during study hall or lunch period, that is optimal. Typically, appointments are scheduled in advance, so it would be advantageous for your student to communicate to their teacher either in person or via email that they will be missing class on that day. Teachers may be able to provide materials ahead of time or can set up a meeting time to review what is missed. Recurring appointments are hard on academic classroom success. If this is unavoidable, reach out to the teacher so that a plan can be put into place to make up for your student's missed class time.

A pattern that has emerged since the pandemic is an avoidance behavior on test/evaluation days. When a student is behind as a result of absences, or as a result of failing to learn the content, anxiety sets in. This type of anxiety seems to stem from the feeling of being unprepared, and the natural response mechanism in that scenario is to avoid. Notice if your student isn't feeling well on test days. Avoidance behavior for one class can begin a chain reaction of being behind in all classes. This quickly creates a hole that some students truly struggle to pull themselves out of. If you notice patterns of "not feeling well" on test days, have a discussion with your student, and open that line of communication with the teacher as well. Together, as a team, establish plans to work through the issues and anxiety that are blocking your student from achieving success.

Long-term absences as a result of illness are challenging for students at this age. The isolation from friends and the routines of school make a complex circumstance even more challenging for students. If your family is in this situation, establish early contact with the school, especially the guidance counselor, as well as your student's teachers. There are many additional supports that school districts can put into place for long-term absence. Depending on the situation, these supports could include extended time to make up assignments, modification of assignments, home tutoring or instruction options, extra support throughout the school day, and/or an IEP or 504 plan to provide appropriate educational support. The school cannot assist if it is not made aware of the need, however. Communication is key.

Finally, family vacation. Many schools have a paperwork process for families to use prior to taking off on vacation, to make sure teachers are aware of the upcoming absence. Students should work to secure relevant course materials prior to their trip and should be prepared to have those materials ready to turn back in upon their return to school. Districts will have different lengths of time that make-up work will be accepted, so familiarize yourself with these guidelines prior to taking your student out of school. Although missing school is hard at any age, in the high school years it is much more difficult to be off for a week and then come back to a week of makeup work along with the week's regular work. If your family is in this situation, it is a great idea to sit down with your student and come up with a plan for how to get their assignments made up in a timely manner. Calendars that allow students to chart and see target dates for completing work are extremely helpful. The ability to physically check off work provides students with a sense that they are making progress in catching up from their absence.

Closing Advice

Help your student establish solid school routines to prevent absences in the first place. Watch how rest, extracurriculars, and good nutrition support your student's success. Little things like relationships and play time may have significant impact on the mind of a freshman student. By establishing healthy routines and opening up lines of communication, students should see that they have a network that they can count on as they navigate this stage of their educational and social journeys. When dealing with absences with your freshman student, dig into the why, be aware of the impact missing a day of school can have, and help nurture and build their ability to advocate for their own needs.

Conversation Starters

- Are there certain teachers you feel as though you can reach out to more than others with questions and concerns? What can you do to feel more comfortable with the others?

- What type of weekly agendas do your teachers provide for you to cross-check if you are absent?

- Which classes create a larger issue if you are absent?

- What can you do if you are feeling overwhelmed when making up work after being absent?

- I've noticed that you seem to not feel well on test days. Do you agree with this observation? Why might this be?

- Can you share an example of how you'll email your teacher when you are absent? Is there a difference in how this will look if you know in advance vs. unexpected absences (like being sick)?

Chapter 13
FINDING PASSIONS...IN AND OUT OF SCHOOL

How to help identify and support your teen's interests

Stacey McAdoo
2019 Arkansas State Teacher of the Year

"Ninth grade is one of the most important years of your high school career" is a phrase I have heard (and said) more times than I can remember. Having spent the overwhelming majority of my professional career teaching freshmen and coordinating the college and career readiness program at Little Rock Central High, I wholeheartedly believe that statement. In fact, when you factor in navigating the transition from middle to high school with learning how to deal with the physical, emotional, and social changes happening to and around 9th graders—in addition to mastering the curriculum and determining which academic and career pathway to traverse—9th grade may very well be one of the most critical years of their life. Period.

Interests and passions play a critical role in the development and success of 9th graders, both in and outside of the classroom. Often, pursuing one's interests and passions results in developing transferable skills that colleges and employers look for, such as self-motivation, a strong work ethic, time management, adaptability, resilience, and leadership. Putting the future benefits aside, finding one's passion also has lots of "right now" appeal. It often creates a sense of purpose and belonging and provides opportunities to help students relax and alleviate stress.

Identifying an Interest

As a parent of two very active children and an educator for 21 years, I have spent more time at school events than I have virtually anywhere else. Each time I facilitate an open house, parent night, or parent-teacher conference, I always share tips on how students can be more successful in my class and throughout their education journey in general. And, although high school is a time when most teenagers begin to crave and ask for more independence, this is an important time for parents to help their child identify their passions and interests, both in and out of school. Listed below are some strategies I have often shared with parents to help them discover their passions and interests.

1. Encourage exploration. Students are never too old to try new things or explore different activities. This can include signing them up for extracurricular activities, summer camps, or classes they have expressed interest in. Encourage them to try different sports, arts, or academic pursuits to see what they enjoy. These pursuits don't have to be competitive. Most schools offer a variety of clubs and intramural sports/activities that students can join. Start there.

2. Listen to your child. Listen carefully to what your child is and isn't saying. Ask open-ended questions and show genuine

interest in what they have to say. This can help your teen feel heard and understood and give you insight into what's going on with them and what they are genuinely interested in.

3. Lead by example. The easiest way to get a child to identify their interests and passions is by sharing your interests and hobbies with them. First, let them see you prioritizing your interests and making time to do something you enjoy. Then, invite them to observe or participate in activities involving your interests and passions.

4. Celebrate successes. When a child discovers a passion or interest, celebrate and encourage them to continue pursuing those interests. This can include attending their performances or events, displaying their artwork or creations, or simply telling them how proud you are of their accomplishments.

5. Be patient. Discovering passions and interests is a process that takes time, so be patient and supportive as your child explores different activities and interests. Try not to pressure your child to find their passion quickly; instead, focus on providing a supportive and nurturing environment for them to explore their interests.

Conversation Starters for Unlocking Your Child's Interests and Passions

Many years ago, I read somewhere that the car was the perfect place to have substantive conversations with teens because, inside a moving vehicle, they are a captive audience. That was hands down one of the best parenting tips I ever discovered. Some of my best conversations with my children have been in the car (with the radio off and phones down). Should you decide to try this parenting hack for yourself, here are some conversation starters to help your child identify their interests and passions:

- What are some things you would do if you had unlimited time and resources?

- Is there a hobby or activity you've always wanted to try?

- What subject do you enjoy most in school?

- What do you think you're good at?

- What's something you've always wanted to learn more about?

These questions will help your child think about their interests and passions and may spark further conversation about their goals and aspirations. It is important to let your child lead the conversation and express their thoughts and ideas without judgment or pressure.

Managing Your Expectations

Helping your child unlock their passions can be exciting and challenging. One of the most important things parents can do during this journey is manage their expectations. Of course, we naturally want our children to share our interests and passions, but it is important to recognize that our children probably will have different interests and desires than we do and that their interests and passions may change over time.

My husband and I develop and facilitate arts integration workshops and professional development for schools and organizations all the time. Classroom management is a topic that is often requested. "You have to plan your discipline just like you plan your lessons" is something my husband says in virtually every session we lead for educators. And the same is true for parenting and trying to help your child discover their interests: You must have a plan. That plan must include strategies to help you manage expectations and support your child's evolving interests and passions.

One of the best ways parents can help support their child is to avoid projecting their own interests onto the child. Instead, parents should listen to their children and support their interests, even if they are different from their own. This can help your teen feel heard and understood and can also help them develop a sense of independence and self-discovery.

Encouraging experimentation with different activities and interests can help your teen discover what they enjoy and are good at. It can also help them develop a sense of curiosity and an openness to new experiences.

Another way to support your child in discovering and developing their interests is to focus on the process, not the outcome. It is important to appreciate the effort and hard work your teen puts into their interests. This can help your teen develop a sense of intrinsic motivation and self-esteem.

We often speak about celebrating diversity when trying to combat discrimination and prejudice. But when we genuinely embrace diversity, we think about it in every aspect of our lives—including our interests and passions, because everyone is unique and has their own strengths and weaknesses. By celebrating diversity, parents can create a positive and accepting environment for their child to explore their interests and passions.

"Change," as Heraclitus (a Greek philosopher) once said, "is the only constant in life." If it is widely accepted that time will change everything and anything, then we must be open to the idea that our child's interests and passions may change over time as the child grows and develops. By being open to change and maintaining a positive attitude, we can support their growth and development in a positive and nurturing way. Doing so will help your teen feel supported and encouraged, even if their interests and passions have changed or are not what you expected.

Finally, seeking advice and support from other parents or professionals who can help you navigate your child's interests and passions can be one of the most effective strategies to help manage expectations and support your child's interests. This can include teachers, coaches, or counselors who can provide guidance and support for both you and your teen.

Children today are experiencing the world quite differently from the generations before them. Many are under tremendous pressure to succeed. Many suffer from the fear of failure. Some need more resources or access to opportunity. And almost all of them experience an enormous number of digital distractions. So when we create a supportive and nurturing environment for our children to explore their interests and passions (while managing our own expectations), we not only help our children develop a sense of purpose and fulfillment that will stay with them throughout their lives, but we also help make our active parenting years more peaceful and pleasant.

The Hidden Costs of Support and Commitment

When a child develops a healthy interest or passion, parents need to support and commit to helping them. This support can come in many forms, including financial, emotional, and physical.

Financial Support

1. Allocate funds. Interests and passions can be expensive. It is helpful to think of exploration and development as an investment. Therefore, allocating a portion of the household budget for equipment, classes, or lessons is wise.

2. Research scholarships. Some interests and passions may require a significant financial investment. However, grants and discounts are often available, even if they are not advertised. So, don't be afraid to ask. You may be surprised at what you discover.

3. Prioritize spending. You can prioritize spending on your child's interests over other discretionary spending. For example, you may forgo a family vacation to pay for your child's summer camp or music lessons.

Emotional Support

1. Show interest. Ask about your teen's progress, attend their performances or games, and provide encouragement and support.

2. Celebrate successes. When your teen accomplishes something related to their interest or passion, recognize their achievements. This can help build their self-esteem and reinforce their commitment to the activity.

3. Provide encouragement. Encourage and support your teen, particularly if they encounter setbacks or challenges related to their interests or passion. This can help them develop resilience and perseverance.

Physical Support

1. Provide or secure transportation. There can be a lot of driving to and from practices, lessons, and events. These activities are rarely canceled because of a long day at work or because it's raining. Therefore, having solid transportation plans is very important.

2. Create space. If possible, create a space in your home where your teen can pursue their interests and passions. It doesn't have to be an entire room if space doesn't permit, but having a designated area/section to spread out materials, and time to practice or engage, helps.

3. Participate. Include yourself in activities related to your teen's interests and passions when possible. This can include

playing sports with them or attending concerts or performances together.

Commitment

1. Make time. Block off time on your calendar to ensure you can support your child's interests and passions.

2. Be consistent. Be consistent in your support of your teen's interests and passions. This can help them develop a sense of stability and appreciate your dependability.

3. Communicate. Talk. Talk some more. Then talk again! Ask your teen about their goals (and periodically ask about their progress toward them) and aspirations related to the activity, and provide guidance and support as needed.

Closing Advice

Identifying interests, managing expectations, and supporting your teen's interests and passions requires a comprehensive approach that includes strategies for discovery, conversation starters, conducting self-assessments, and being committed. Exploring and developing one's interests and passions can take time. But, in the end, the patience, commitment, and resources devoted to it are worth it when a parent is able to see a return on their investment by witnessing their child develop a sense of self-esteem, resilience, and a love of learning. Your support and commitment to your teen's interests and passions can profoundly impact their well-being and success in life.

Self-Assessment

Checklists and self-assessments are two tools that help me tremendously in the classroom, as a parent, and in my day-to-day life. Here are a few questions that can be asked to help you manage your own expectations when trying to help your child discover or identify their interests and passions:

- Am I open to my child's interests even if they differ from mine?

- Am I allowing my child to explore their interests without trying to push them in a certain direction?

- Am I putting too much pressure on my child to find their passion or achieve success in a certain area?

- Am I allowing my child to make and learn from mistakes?

- Do I understand that my child's interests and passions may change over time?

- Am I providing my child a supportive environment to explore their interests and passions?

- Am I listening to my child's thoughts and ideas without dismissing or minimizing them?

- Am I focusing on my child's strengths and encouraging them to develop those areas?

- Am I celebrating my child's successes, no matter how small?

- Am I remembering that my child's journey of self-discovery is their own and not something I can control or dictate?

Parents can gain insight into their expectations and attitudes toward their child's interests and passions by asking these questions. This self-reflection can help parents approach the process of helping their children discover and identify their interests in a supportive and positive way.

Chapter 14

HOW WILL I KNOW IF MY CHILD IS READY FOR 10TH GRADE?

Expert advice for preparing your
student for sophomore year

Carolyn Kielma
2023 Connecticut State Teacher of the Year

Hopefully, your child has found new independence during their first year of high school, but if not, what to do? How do you help them prepare for honors and AP (Advanced Placement), IB (International Baccalaureate), PLTW (Project Lead the Way), or other courses that have the option for students to earn college/university credits while balancing extracurricular and outside activities?

Making the Decision to Enroll in AP/IB Courses

Likely in the spring of your child's freshman year, they selected courses for their sophomore year. This can be an exciting time, as they are finally allowed to choose classes that interest them after taking the same courses as their peers for their entire educational career up until now. It is normal for your child to want to take *all* of the advanced courses offered to avoid FOMO (fear of missing out).

As a sophomore biology teacher for more than 20 years, I have seen this firsthand. I encourage you to ask your child to list all of the courses that interest them, and then prioritize them. Often, students take on more than they can handle. They take classes because they "are good at them" and not because they are truly interested or invested in the coursework. I find that the students who are most successful are the ones who choose only *one* high-level course (AP or IB) in their sophomore year. Once they are familiar with the high expectations, rigor, and homework demands, they can then make an informed decision about what to take during their junior and senior years. The student who is "good at" geometry but doesn't really enjoy the content should not consider taking AP Statistics as a sophomore.

You might be tempted to push your child to be the best they can be. This is completely understandable, as you know how bright and capable your child is, but I encourage you to take it slow. There is so much social and emotional learning that must take place during the adolescent years, and overburdening a child with coursework, projects, and homework by overscheduling advanced classes can take away from extracurricular activities and sports and be detrimental to mental health.

The Summer Before Sophomore Year

Wow! You made it through freshman year! Kudos for keeping it together and getting this far. Each year in high school provides its own unique challenges, but freshman year can definitely be the most confusing and overwhelming for adolescents and parents. More freedom and responsibility can be tricky to prioritize, but somehow you made it.

Now that you and your child have chosen the AP course that suits them best, you can relax and enjoy the summer, right? Well, yes and no. Prior to sophomore year, it may be in your child's best interest to continue learning during the summer. According to research done by the *Washington Post*, students can lose between two and two-and-a-half months of math skills from the previous year's learning. This "brain drain" happens for all children, regardless of their economic, social, or ethnic background. Reading comprehension can also take a hit, especially for students who come from lower socioeconomic backgrounds. Students can lose up to three months of reading skills in just two to three months of summer break.

The vacation learning loss may be detrimental for high school students who hope to take accelerated, honors, AP, or other college credit-level courses. With these high-demand academic requirements, your child cannot afford to lose two to three months of academic progress. Fortunately, research has also shown that brain drain can be reversed if children participate in meaningful learning over the summer.

Some advanced courses may provide a summer packet to prepare students for fall coursework. If this is the case, encourage your child to start that work. This can allow you and your child to see what they are getting into. Remind your child that this is the first impression the teacher will get of their work, so they should take extra time and effort to complete it. In many cases, that work may be work that your student is expected to know prior to day one of school. For example, the summer packet at my school for AP Biology has historically been all about laboratory safety, protocol, and equipment, something the state requires students to know and understand before beginning any laboratory work.

If there is no summer packet or pre-course work, there is still learning that can prepare your student for any advanced course. There are so many ways to incorporate learning within fun activities that can be interesting and exciting for your child and possibly your family as a whole. At this age, there may be some resentment if you even mention the terms "summer" and "homework" in the same paragraph, so be mindful of the activities you mention and steer clear of forcing too much work on your child, who may genuinely need a break from the rigors of the classroom.

If your student does truly enjoy learning and academics, you can certainly look at sites like Khan Academy (https://www.khanacademy .org/), AP Practice Exams (https://www.appracticeexams.com/), or Kaplan test prep (https://www.kaptest.com/ap/free/ap-practice). The College Board (https://www.collegeboard.org/) also provides a personal, detailed, and comprehensive list of what your child should focus on studying if they took the PSAT test during freshman year.

There are many non-technology-related opportunities that will foster growth and maintain learning without being overwhelming. Consider volunteering with your child at a local food bank, community service organization, church, or soup kitchen. Not only will this help them contribute to their community, but it also allows students to learn and grow by immersing themselves in something they may initially feel uncomfortable about. Stepping out of their comfort zone may lead to new opportunities, as they learn to meet new people, communicate with people they may otherwise never have encountered, become leaders, work within a team, discover new places and/or resources available to them, and perhaps even test out possible career fields. Mastering some of these skills will be useful when they are faced with difficult coursework and need to reach out for help.

If volunteering is not an option, consider day trips to local art museums, science centers, war or history museums, open-air theaters, or maritime centers or aquariums. Create a well-rounded student who is not afraid to take risks by going on day hikes, enjoying trips to the nature center at the closest beach, or even speaking to park rangers at your state or national park. Encourage exploration and adventures outside of your comfort zone, as well. This will help you make connections with your child, which will be important when the stress of the school year comes.

It is also important to encourage your rising sophomore to read for at least 20 minutes a day. This can be a book of their choice or a graphic novel, magazine, newspaper, self-help book, or online biography. Again, variety is the key to exposing them to the various genres of literature they may encounter in AP or IB coursework. The graphic below emphasizes the importance of this daily routine.

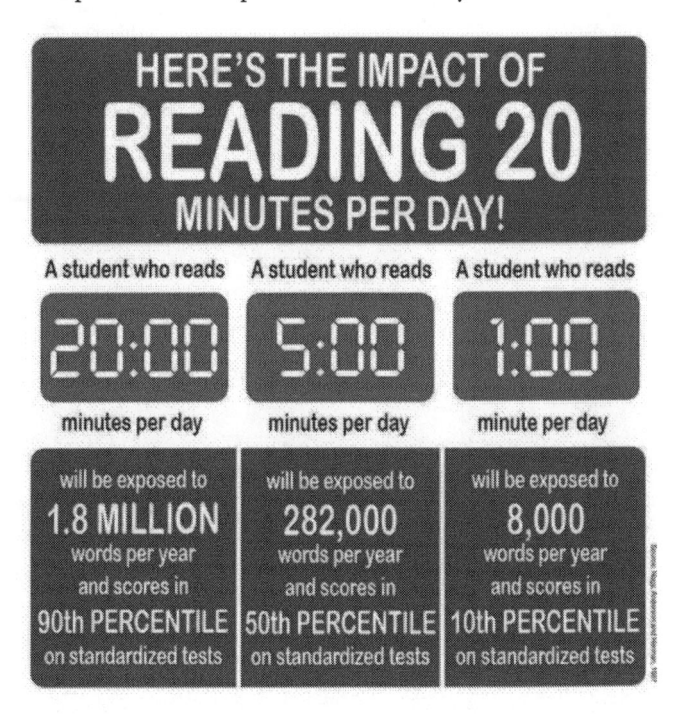

Sophomore Year is a Big Jump! How Else Can We Prepare?

Besides an adventurous yet restful summer, your child will also need to prepare for the organizational rigors of advanced coursework. Reach out to the teacher to get the required course materials before the summer begins, if you are able. Many teachers will distribute textbooks before the end of freshman year or share websites and electronic resources that you may need to create accounts and passwords for. Trying to do all of that in the first week of school may be daunting, and your student will be relieved to get that already settled before the studying and coursework begins.

To avoid being a "helicopter parent," it is good to teach your student how to draft a professional email to a teacher. Review "5 Things to Consider When Emailing Your Teacher" provided by Grammarly at https://www.grammarly.com/blog/email-teacher/ for help. Explain to your child that emailing the teacher over the summer lets that educator know how seriously you take the course. It allows them to know that you have drive and determination and are excited about the course.

Even if not specifically listed on the syllabus, a good resource for students is always a sturdy paper planner. While many students say they will just "make a note in my phone" or "set a reminder for Siri or Alexa," a 2021 University of Tokyo study shows stronger brain activity after writing on paper than on a tablet or smartphone, and a *New York Times* article titled "The Case for Using a Paper Planner" states that "writing by hand forces you to slow down and approach your planning with more mindfulness and helps you retain information better," which is extremely important for building strong and successful work habits.

Okay, Class Has Begun: Now What?

So you have made it to day one of sophomore year. What can your child do so they can stay on top of the workload and not fall behind? The most obvious answer is to stress the importance of good attendance, communicating with teachers, and following through, especially if absences do occur. Remind your child to email or reach out to teachers prior to absences if you are able or as soon as possible to create a schedule for making up work or meeting with the teacher to get the work that was missed. Students will *always* have homework. Even if there is no assigned reading, worksheet, or report due, the student should review their notes and check their understanding of concepts after each class and prior to the next one. They should practice good planning, time management, and study skills, including learning to pace themselves during long-term projects.

The first accelerated-level courses may also require that your child increase their study time or reinvent the way they take notes. Students must learn to take notes that work for them and use those notes to study effectively. This is not a one-size-fits-all situation, because there are many ways to take notes and each method has benefits, depending on how your child's brain processes information. Check out *How to Take Better Notes: The 6 Best Note-Taking Systems* by Elizabeth Lundin for more information.

You should be prepared to exercise a new level of patience and understanding, as well. Know that many advanced courses like AP and IB are weighted courses. This means that your child's grades may not always reflect the A student you may be used to. With the increased rigor, those As may become Bs or even Cs. The "weight" of a course may mean that mathematically the course increases the student's overall GPA. Trust your school counselor when they tell you that a college or university will be more in favor of a student challenging themselves with an accelerated or college course and earning a B or C, than a student in a regular level course who earns an A. Try to be flexible with your expectations of your student's performance, and reach out directly to the teacher if you have any questions or concerns.

Closing Advice

Trust that your student knows what to do, but also be mindful of any mental health struggles or signs of overwork and stress. You can be the best source of support for them, but hovering and being too demanding may push them away. They are doing their best to navigate high school, and you may both need to exercise extreme patience and understanding. Try to keep the lines of communication open, and you should both learn a lot this year. You've got this!

Conversation Starters

- What are your summer plans for getting ready for your higher-level courses in the fall?

- How will you organize your time to fit classwork in with your extracurricular activities?

- What does the course syllabus say about the amount of work and the time needed to complete it weekly?

- How will you contact your teacher if you need help or clarification on a topic or assignment?

- What is the best way for you to take notes on a topic? How do you use those notes to study?

36807885R00093